India's Phytonutrient Report

ABOUT THE AUTHORS:

Arpita Mukherjee is a Professor at Indian Council for Research on International Economic Relations (ICRIER). She has several years of experience in policy-oriented research, working closely with the government in India and policymakers in the EU, US, ASEAN and in East Asian countries. She has conducted studies for international organisations and Indian industry associations. Her research is a key contributor to India's negotiating strategies in the WTO and bilateral agreements. She has authored chapters in joint study group reports set up by Indian government and has led research teams contributing to India's domestic policy reforms in areas such as logistics, retail, special economic zones and mega food parks. Dr Mukherjee has a PhD in Economics from the University of Portsmouth, UK. She has published widely and presented her research in various international and national forums.

Souvik Dutta is an Assistant Professor in Economics at Indian Institute of Management Bangalore (IIMB) and is the recipient of the Young Faculty Research Chair at IIMB. He has published in reputed journals and his primary research interests lie in the areas of Applied Microeconomics, Development and Political Economy. He has been an active researcher in survey-based studies related to policy and planning. He has worked on express delivery services in India in collaboration with ICRIER, which involved extensive primary survey of express and courier companies and identifying barriers and making policy suggestions. Other major projects involve studying microfinance in West Bengal, which is funded by International Growth Center, London School of Economics. Prof Dutta holds a PhD in Economics from Pennsylvania State University, USA and a Masters in Economics from Delhi School of Economics.

Tanu M. Goyal is a Consultant at ICRIER. Her research interests include trade in services, food supply chain, international trade agreements and policy and regulatory issues. She has been working at ICRIER since 2008 and has worked on projects for the Government of India, Asian Development Bank (ADB), European Commission (EC), Konrad-Adenauer-Stiftung (KAS), Indian Institute of Management (IIM), Italian Trade Commission, among others. She has contributed to policy reports for the Indian government as well international agencies. She has extensively worked on international agreements and has authored reports providing negotiating strategy for the bilateral agreements being negotiated by the Indian government. She has co-edited a book on trade agreements and has also published several international and national journal articles, book chapters, reports and other popular media articles on policy issues. She holds a Masters degree in Economics with specialisation in world economy, from Centre of Trade and Development (CITD), Jawaharlal Nehru University, New Delhi.

India's Phytonutrient Report

A Snapshot of Fruits and Vegetables Consumption, Availability and Implications for Phytonutrient Intake

ACADEMIC FOUNDATION
NEW DELHI

www.academicfoundation.org

First published in 2016
by

ACADEMIC FOUNDATION
4772-73 / 23 Bharat Ram Road, (23 Ansari Road),
Darya Ganj, New Delhi - 110 002 (India).
Phones : 23245001 / 02 / 03 / 04.
Fax : +91-11-23245005.
E-mail : books@academicfoundation.com
www.academicfoundation.com

and

INDIAN COUNCIL FOR RESEARCH ON INTERNATIONAL ECONOMIC RELATIONS (ICRIER)
Core 6A, 4th Floor India Habitat Centre, Lodhi Road, New Delhi 110003

Opinions and recommendations in the report are exclusively of the author(s) and not of any other individual or institution including ICRIER. This report has been prepared in good faith on the basis of information available at the date of publication. All interactions and transactions with industry sponsors and their representatives have been transparent and conducted in an open, honest and independent manner as enshrined in ICRIER Memorandum of Association. ICRIER does not accept any corporate funding that comes with a mandated research area which is not in line with ICRIER's research agenda. The corporate funding of an ICRIER activity does not, in any way, imply ICRIER's endorsement of the views of the sponsoring organization or its products or policies. ICRIER does not conduct research that is focused on any specific product or service provided by the corporate sponsor.

India's Phytonutrient Report: A Snapshot of Fruits and Vegetables Consumption, Availability and Implications for Phytonutrient Intake.

by Arpita Mukherjee, Souvik Dutta and Tanu M. Goyal

ISBN 9789332703537

Typeset, printed and bound by The Book Mint, New Delhi.
www.thebookmint.in

Contents

List of Tables, Figures, Boxes and Appendices

Tables

Figures

Boxes

Appendices

Foreword

India is one of the largest producers of fruits and vegetables in the world. It is also one of the largest consumer markets in the world, with consumption constituting around 59 per cent of GDP. Food and grocery have the largest share in the consumption basket. It is well known that consumption patterns are affected by both demand and supply side factors. With increase in income, the composition of the food basket is changing from cereals and pulses to fruits, vegetables, milk and milk products and meat. Further, consumption is also determined by the price, availability and quality of produce.

As laymen, everybody is aware of the benefits of consuming fruits and vegetables. However, a pioneering study by the World Health Organization (WHO) panel on diet, nutrition and prevention of chronic diseases has recommended that the daily intake of at least 400 grams of fruits and vegetables, excluding potatoes, cassava and other starchy tubers, helps prevent diet-related chronic diseases and micronutrient deficiencies. Fruits and vegetables are essential sources of phytonutrients, which promote a range of health benefits. Different combinations of fruits and vegetables provide different types of phytonutrients.

Existing studies on the Indian consumption pattern by the WHO and different Indian organisations highlight that Indian consumers do not consume the recommended quantity of fruits and vegetables. Secondary data also shows that while India is one of the largest producers of fruits and vegetables, productivity is low. Moreover, while the country is a net importer of fruits and vegetables and there is growing demand, there are import restrictions. Besides, the fruits and vegetables supply chain is fragmented and there is high incidence of wastage, resulting in sporadic shortages and increase in prices. All these factors affect access to fruits and vegetables and its consumption.

Besides, while there are a number of regulations governing the food supply chain sector, the regulatory framework is weak as regulations are still evolving and their implementation is sketchy. There is hardly any traceability from farm to fork—the quality of fruits and vegetables and the insecticides and pesticides used in their production have raised concerns about the health of Indians. All these issues affect the consumption of fruits and vegetables in the country. While consumers can cover the nutritional deficiencies by consuming health supplements and nutraceuticals, in India, the regulations on nutraceuticals are evolving and intake of health supplements is low.

Given this background, this study examines the consumption of fruits and vegetables patterns for Indian consumers, identifies the shortfall in consumptions, examines the reasons for such shortfall and makes policy recommendations. The report is based on a primary survey of 1001 consumers and analysis of secondary data. The study reveals some striking findings. The present level of consumption of fruits and vegetables across middle and high income urban consumers is much lower than the WHO recommended quality. Income, diet pattern, lifestyle, prices, etc., play an important role in determining the intake of fruits and vegetables. Further, young Indians are more likely to fall short of the WHO recommended consumption compared to adults. This is a cause for concern as the health of its youth determines the growth and development of a nation like India, which currently enjoys a young demographic profile that can be potentially transformative. Moreover, the survey participants have raised concerns about the quality of produce. They would like to access organic products but they have limited choice in terms of the type of produce they want and in the format that they want it (chopped, frozen, packed, etc.). These findings raise the question of whether Indian consumers have been ignored in policymaking. Are we doing enough to have a healthy nation? How can the policy help, guide consumers into a better diet pattern? What should be done to increase consumers' access to fruits and vegetables and their awareness of the benefits of consuming fruits and vegetables? What should be the right policy to have a win-win situation for farmers, producers and consumers? This report tries to answer these questions.

The report will enable producers to understand the consumers' consumption patterns, companies to understand the regulatory environment for fruits and vegetables supply chain, policy makers to understand the demand and supply gaps and areas of policy intervention, and most important, it will raise awareness among consumers about the benefits of consuming fruits and vegetables.

We gratefully acknowledge the support of the Amway Opportunity Foundation, who sponsored this study, and our survey partner, Spectrum Research Group, for conduction the survey within a short period. The authors of this report have been working closely with different departments of the government on streamlining the food supply chain and I do hope that the findings of the report will provide valuable inputs into policymaking.

— Rajat Kathuria

Director and Chief Executive,
Indian Council for Research on
International Economic Relations (ICRIER)

Acknowledgements

We express our gratitude to Rajat Kathuria, Director and Chief Executive, ICRIER, for giving us the opportunity to work in this area and for his constant support. We would like to thank Amway Opportunity Foundation for sponsoring this study. We are especially grateful to Rajat Banerji and John L. Khiangte for their support and valuable inputs during the course of this project. Pallab Ghosh and his team at Spectrum Research Group deserve a special mention for conducting the consumer survey. We are grateful to all survey participants for taking time off from their busy schedule to fill up the questionnaire and for their inputs. We would like to thank Suvi Agrawal and Avantika Kapoor, our project interns, for their valuable contribution to this project. Thanks are due to Bhavook Bhardwaj for his help in compiling the report and Sahil Gandhi for his help in the pilot survey.

We would like to thank Tara Nair for copyediting. The administrative team of ICRIER deserves a special mention. In particular, we would like to thank Anu Mohandas, Chhaya Singh, Aric Mary, Hilda Kathuria, Anshul Bhijwani, Raj Kumar Shahi, Rajeev Kapil and his team and Manmeet Ahuja and his team.

Last but not the least, we would like to thank Academic Foundation, especially Sanu Kapila and Sona Kapila, for publishing the report within a short time frame.

List of Abbreviations

APMC	Agricultural Produce and Marketing Committee
ARS	Agricultural Research Service
ASEAN	Association of South East Asian Nations
CAGR	Compound Annual Growth Rate
CECA	Comprehensive Economic Cooperation Agreement
CEPA	Comprehensive Economic Partnership Agreement
DGFT	Directorate General of Foreign Trade
EIC	Export Inspection Council
EU	European Union
FAO	Food and Agriculture Organization
FDI	Foreign Direct Investment
FIPB	Foreign Investment Promotion Board
FSSA	Food Safety and Standards Act
FSSAI	Food Safety and Standards Authority of India
GDP	Gross Domestic Product
HA	Hectare
IMF	International Monetary Fund
ITC-HS	Indian Trade Clarification based on Harmonised System of Coding
MPCE	Monthly Per Capita Expenditure
MRL	Maximum Residue Level
MT	Metric Tonne
NABARD	National Bank for Agriculture and Rural Development
NCAER	National Council of Applied Economic Research
NCCP	National Codex Contact Point
NCR	National Capital Region
NSS	National Sample Survey
NSSO	National Sample Survey Organisation
SEC	Socio-Economic Classification
SEZs	Special Economic Zones
SPS	Sanitary and Phytosanitary
TBT	Technical Barriers to Trade
UAE	United Arab Emirates
UN	United Nations
US	United States
USDA	United States Department of Agriculture
WHO	World Health Organization
WHS	World Health Survey
WPI	Wholesale Price Index
YoY	Year-on-Year

Introduction

India is one of the fastest growing economies in the world. In the period between 2000 and 2014, the Indian economy has grown at an average annual growth rate of 7.02 per cent.[1] According to the International Monetary Fund (IMF), India will outgrow China (growth projected at 6.3 per cent) with a GDP growth rate of 7.5 per cent during the period of 2015-16. This GDP growth is primarily due to increase in domestic demand, arising from a rise in per capita income and a fast growing middle income group, commonly called the middle-class.[2] According to Credit Suisse (2015), with a middle-class population of about 23.6 million people, India ranks 8th among 215 countries in terms of the number of middle-class adults in 2015. McKinsey & Company (2007) predicted that if the Indian economy grows at 7.3 per cent between 2005 and 2025, the share of the middle class in the population will increase from 5 per cent to 41 per cent, and it is this group that will drive future demand and consumption patterns in India.

Focusing specifically on consumption, the World Bank estimates that 59.2 per cent of the Indian GDP was consumed in 2013, which is higher than in China (34.1 per cent). India is expected to be the 5th largest consumer market by 2025, if current growth rates continue.[3] Food and grocery constitute a substantial part of India's consumption basket. Out of total private final consumption expenditure, about 28 per cent was on food alone and around 30 per cent on food and beverage combined in 2013-14.[4] This compares to only 9 per cent in the United States (US), 17 per cent in Brazil and 25 per cent in China.[5]

India will outgrow China (growth projected at 6.3 per cent) with a GDP growth rate of 7.5 per cent during the period of 2015-16.

With increase in incomes, the composition of the food basket is likely to change from cereals and pulses to fruits, vegetables, milk and milk products and meat. Consumption is also affected by supply side factors such as a rise in production or the removal of barriers to trade. It is likely that with liberalisation, globalisation and easing out of trade restrictions, different types of fresh and processed food will be more readily available in the country. Today, fruits and vegetables are available in different forms such as fresh, frozen, juices and chopped, through multiple retail channels such as push carts, mom-and-pop stores, supermarket and online retail and in different product categories (branded and non-branded, organic and non-organic, etc.), which has widened the choice available to consumers.

India is expected to be the fifth largest consumer market by 2025, if the current growth continues.

Food and beverage accounted for 30 per cent of the total private final consumption expenditure in 2013-14.

In spite of these positive developments, a number of studies show that Indians are falling short of their calorie intake or the "recommended" nutritional requirements. For example, a survey conducted by the National Sample Survey Organisation (NSSO)[6] on the *Nutritional Intake in India (2011-12)* found that, since the year 2000, there has been a sharp decline in calorie intake in both urban and rural India resulting in low nutrition levels. It was further found that in India more than 50 per cent of the calories and nutrition are derived from cereals rather than non-cereal products such as fruits and vegetables. On an average, fruits and vegetables contributed to only around 9 per cent of the calorie intake. Another study of a sample of 10,750 households from six states (Assam, Karnataka, Maharashtra, Rajasthan, Uttar Pradesh and West Bengal) shows that 78 per cent of respondents reported insufficient intake of fruits and vegetables.[7] The Integrated Disease Surveillance

1. Data extracted from International Monetary Fund (IMF). *http://www.imf.org/external/pubs/ft/weo/2015/01/weodata/weorept.aspx?sy=2000&ey=2014&scsm=1&ssd=1&sort=country&ds=.&br=1&pr1.x=58&pr1.y=10&c=534&s=NGDP_RPCH&grp=0&a=#cs1* (accessed on 22 November 2015).
2. The National Council for Applied Economic Research (NCAER) defines the Indian middle-class as the income group with an annual household income in the range of INR 200,000 to INR 1 million per annum (Shukla, 2010).
3. McKinsey & Company (2007).
4. Images Multimedia Private Limited (2015).
5. The Boston Consulting Group (2012).
6. For details see (NSSO, 2014). The survey covered about 203,313 households in both rural and urban areas and the information was collected during 2011-12.
7. WHO (2003).

Project (IDSP) of the Ministry of Health and Family Welfare selected a sample of 5,000 households from seven states (Andhra Pradesh, Kerala, Madhya Pradesh, Maharashtra, Mizoram, Tamil Nadu and Uttarakhand) between 2007 and 2008 and found that a high proportion of population takes inadequate amounts of fruits and vegetables. Marginal differences were observed across age groups, levels of education, occupation and residence.[8] The broad conclusion from all these surveys is that there is lack of adequate intake of fruits and vegetables in India.

Given this background, it is important to understand the paradox—the shortfall in nutrients and consumption of fruits and vegetables despite a rise in incomes. The key issue is how can the shortfall, if it exists, be addressed so that the health of the nation is not compromised. This requires an analysis of both demand and supply side factors. Supply side factors such as the seasonality of production, fragmented supply chain, etc., have largely been ignored in the survey-based studies discussed above. This report aims to fill that lacuna.

In India, more than 50 per cent of the calories and nutrition are derived from cereals rather than non-cereal products such as fruits and vegetables.

The layout of the report is as follows.

- Section 1 provides a snapshot of why fruits and vegetables are important in our diet, what is the WHO recommended daily intake of fruits and vegetables and the benefits of consuming the same.
- Section 2 presents a typical supply chain for fruits and vegetables. It examines production, trade and overall availability of fruits and vegetables. It also presents consumption patterns and the prices of fruits and vegetables.
- Section 3 provides an in-depth analysis of the regulations that affect the supply and consumption of fruits and vegetables.
- Section 4 analyses demand-side factors. Based on a primary survey of 1,001 consumers across five states, it highlights their consumption and purchase behaviour, shortfall in consumption if any, reasons for the shortfall, etc.

The objective of this report is to understand the 'actual' consumption of fruits and vegetables in India and compare this to the WHO 'recommended' quantity for an adult. It also examines the reasons for the shortfall wherever they exist and makes policy recommendations.

- Section 5 presents the demand side and supply side barriers leading to a shortfall in consumption of fruits and vegetables.
- Section 6 summarises the key findings of the report and makes policy recommendations.

8. National Institute of Medical Statistics, Indian Council of Medical Research (ICMR) (2009).

1

Benefits of Consumption of Fruits and Vegetables

Globally, there are several studies highlighting the benefits of consumption of fruits and vegetables. This section summarises the findings of global studies and studies conducted in India.

1.1 Global Studies

Fruits and vegetables contain "phytonutrients", which promote a range of health benefits (see Box 1.1 for definition). The World Health Organization (WHO) panel on diet, nutrition and prevention of chronic diseases recommended a daily intake of at least 400 grams (or five daily servings with an average serving size of 80 gm) of fruits and vegetables, excluding potatoes, cassava and other starchy tubers, to prevent include 5 carotenoids (alpha-carotene, beta-carotene, beta-cryptoxanthin, lutein/zeaxanthin, lycopene) and 4 polyphenols, comprising 3 flavonoids (anthocyanidins, hesperetin, quercetin), and 1 non-flavanoid (ellagic acid).[2] A number of studies show that certain fruits and vegetables are rich in certain phytonutrients.[3] Table 1.1 provides a description of various fruits and vegetables, their phytonutrient content and the health benefits from the consumption of selected fruits and vegetables. The table provides groups or combination of fruits and vegetables that give similar benefits. Hence, a consumer can choose between fruits and vegetables in a group and meet the nutrient requirements.

Box 1.1

Definition of Phytonutrients

The term "phyto" originated from a Greek word meaning plant. Unlike traditional nutrients (protein, fat, vitamins, and minerals), phytonutrients are not "essential" for life. However, they promote a range of health benefits for the eye, bone and heart as well as support immunity and brain functions.*

WHO Recommended Daily Intake of Fruits and Vegetables

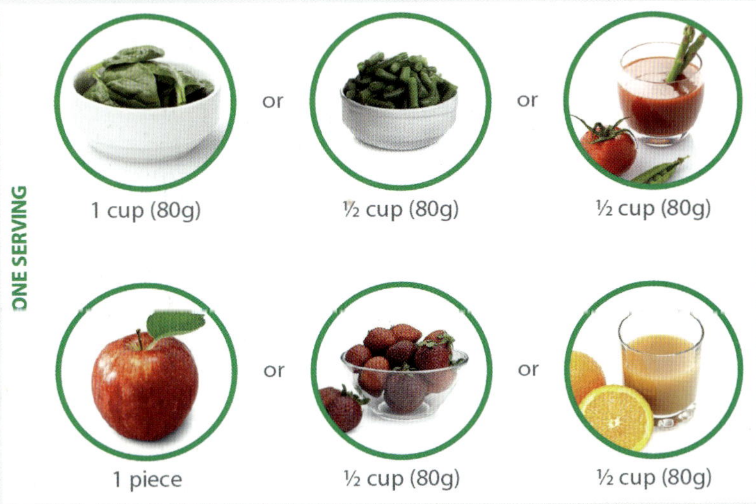

Source: * United States Department of Agriculture (USDA), Agricultural Research Service (ARS).

diet-related chronic diseases and micronutrient deficiencies.[1]

Existing research show that there are more than 600 phytonutrients; however nutrition research has focused primarily on 9 phytonutrients. These

There are a number of medical studies that specifically highlight the benefits of different types of phytonutrients.[4] For example, carotenoids (in

1. WHO (2003).

2. Murphy et al. (2012).

3. Liu (2013) and Beecher (1999).

4. For details, see Khan et al. (2010), Joseph et al. (2009), Morand et al. (2011), Son et al. (2008), Aiyer et al. (2008) and Steinmetz and Potter (1996).

particular, beta-carotene) reduce the risk of heart disease.[5] Flavonoids with their anti-inflammatory characteristics can protect against cancer and cardiovascular disease.[6] Lutein and zeaxanthin help to reduce the effects of oxidative injury that contribute to the development of age-related macular degeneration.[7]

Considering this, several international organisations and countries have undertaken studies to examine the consumption of phytonutrients and food products rich in phytonutrients, globally and in select markets. The most well-known survey based study is that of the WHO, which is a World Health Survey (WHS) of over 300,000 individuals aged 18 years and above in 70 countries between 2002 and 2004. In this study, respondents were grouped according to geographic diet clusters, using the recall method for intake. It was found that the vast majority of adults (58-88 per cent) worldwide consume less than the minimum of five servings of fruits and vegetables per day.[8] Taking this survey as the base, the Nutrilite Health Institute (2014) in the Global Phytonutrient Report pointed out that those consuming low amounts and varieties of fruits and vegetables are also likely to consume low quantities and varieties of phytonutrients. The report also mentioned that a majority of adults would need to at least double their current intake to meet the minimum WHO recommendations. The study refers to some of the barriers related to low consumption of fruits and vegetables, which include the busy lifestyle of consumers, cost, and the seasonal and geographic availability of fruits and vegetables,[9] but does not describe them in detail.

A dietary study conducted by Murphy et al. (2012) in the US using the recall method for dietary intake found that energy adjusted intakes of all phytonutrients were higher among adults whose diets conform to the dietary guidance for fruit and vegetables. Another study showed that each increment of three daily servings of fruits and vegetables reduced the risk of stroke by 22 per cent.[10]

5. Mente et al. (2009).
6. Garcia-Lafuente et al. (2009).
7. Olson et al. (2011).
8. Murphy et. al. (2012).
9. Available at: *http://www.amway.com/lcl/en/ResourceCenter Documents/Visitor/nutr-nut-fact-v-en--GlobalPhytonutrient ReportFAQ.pdf* (accessed on 23 November 2015).
10. Gillman et al.(1995).

1.2 Indian Diet Pattern and Consumption of Fruits and Vegetables

As discussed in the previous section, a number of studies show that there are nutritional deficiencies in the Indian diet and the consumption of fruits and vegetable is low. The NSSO (2014) study on *Nutritional Intake in India (2011-12)* covering about 203,313 households in both rural villages and urban blocks shows that there are state-wise variations in the consumption of different food articles and hence, nutritional intake. However, on an average, the Indian diet pattern is skewed towards cereals with fruits and vegetables accounting for only 9 per cent of calorie intake. Within non-cereals, most of the calories are drawn from oil, fat, and milk and milk products as opposed to fruits and vegetables.

> On an average, the Indian diet pattern is skewed towards cereals with fruits and vegetables accounting for only 9 per cent of calorie intake.

While consumption patterns vary across states, there exist some common trends in consumption across the country. The typical Indian diet is rice or wheat based, with lentils, vegetables, meat and other proteins as supplements. Potato, onion and tomato among vegetables and banana among fruits form a major component of the Indian consumption basket. The most distinguishing feature of the Indian diet, as highlighted in the Phytonutrient Report on Asian countries (Nutrilite Health Institute, 2015), is its high content of spices such as ginger, turmeric, etc., which are rich sources of phytonutrients.

Another study conducted by the Institute of Health Metrics and Evaluations[11] revealed that in 2013, in terms of the disability adjusted life years, dietary risks were the leading risk factors in the country. Further, it was also found that the low intake of fruits and vegetables was a key risk factor in India.

Given the benefits of consuming fruits and vegetables, we now look at the supply chain of fruits and vegetables, covering production, trade and distribution and pricing.

11. The information is based on more than 50,000 different data sources, which researchers have used to produce the most scientifically rigorous estimates possible. For details see *http://www.healthdata.org/india* (accessed on 3 December 2015).

Table 1.1

Phytonutrient Content in Select Fruits, Vegetables and Spices

Food Type	*Group*	*Samples Included*	*Nutrient Content*	*Benefit*
Vegetables	Fruiting vegetables (including melons)	Tomato, green chillies, eggplant, okra, pumpkin, gourds, cucumber, green pepper, *parval/patal*	Rich sources of phytonutrients such as carotenoid lycopene, alpha and beta carotene. Additionally deliver anthocyanidin and phenolic compounds	Protective for eye health, especially for the ageing population. Also promote cell health, heart health and bone health
	Brassica vegetables	Cauliflower, cabbage, broccoli	Good sources of phytonutrients such as beta carotene	Important for heart health and vision health
	Leafy vegetables	Spinach, cilantro, others (indigenous varieties)	Rich sources of phytonutrients such as beta carotene, quercitin and active phenolic acid compounds	Promote eye health, control of blood sugar level and lower lipid levels
	Root, bulb or tuberous vegetables	Potato, onion, garlic, carrots, radish	High starch or insulin content Rich sources of phytonutrients such as anthocyanins, quercetin, phenolics and carotenoids	Promote digestive heath, bone health, and vision health, along with anti-inflammatory, anti-bacterial and anti-arthritis properties
Fruits	Tropical and subtropical fruits	Bananas, mangoes, papayas, guavas, pineapples	Good sources of vitamins A, C and E as well as phytonutrients (alpha and beta carotene, beta-cryptoxanthin and lycopene)	Important for maintaining eye health, bone health
	Citrus fruits	Oranges, lemons and limes, *kinnow*	Rich sources of vitamins C and phytonutrients (hesperidin, beta-cryptoxanthin and lycopene)	Lipid lowering properties. Supports prostate and lung health
	Pome and stone fruits	Apples, pears, peaches, plums	Sources of phytonutrients such as quercetin and beta-carotene	Important for maintaining heart health
	Melons	Watermelons, cantaloupes	Deliver phytonutrients such as lycopene and beta carotene	Promote healthy growth and development
	Berries	Grapes, gooseberries ('*amla*'), strawberries, mulberry	Excellent sources of phytonutrient anthocyanidin	Promote cell health, skin health and digestive health
Spices	Permanent spice crops	Ginger, turmeric	Deliver natural phenolic compounds such as curcuminoids (curcumin, gingerols) and carotenoids	Relax digestive tract, promote cell health, inhibit tumour formation and have anti-inflammatory properties

Note: Classification is done in accordance with the Nutrilite Health Institute (2014) and Food and Agriculture Organization (FAO) (2015).[13]

Source: USDA.

13. *http://www.fao.org/es/faodef/faodefe.htm* (accessed on 23 November 2015).

2

The Supply, Consumption and Prices of Fruits and Vegetables

A typical supply chain for fruits and vegetables in India is characterised by the presence of a number of small players and multiple intermediaries. The average size of land holding in 2010-11 was 1.16 hectares[1] while around 90 per cent of the players in the cold chain sector are in the non-corporate sector with one to two cold storages or refrigerated vehicles. There are very few pan-India integrated cold chain service providers. The aggregators and large farmers collect the produce from small and medium-size farmers and very few farmers sell the produce directly to processors or retailers. The share of the corporate or organised food retailers in total food retail business was only 1.6 per cent in 2013-14.[2] Even organised retailers primarily source fresh fruits and vegetables from the *mandis* or aggregators. There are only a few instances of direct sourcing from farmers. Figure 2.1 presents the typical supply chain for fruits and vegetables. The domestic availability of fruits and vegetables depends on domestic production and imports.

Figure 2.1

A Typical Supply Chain for Fruits and Vegetables

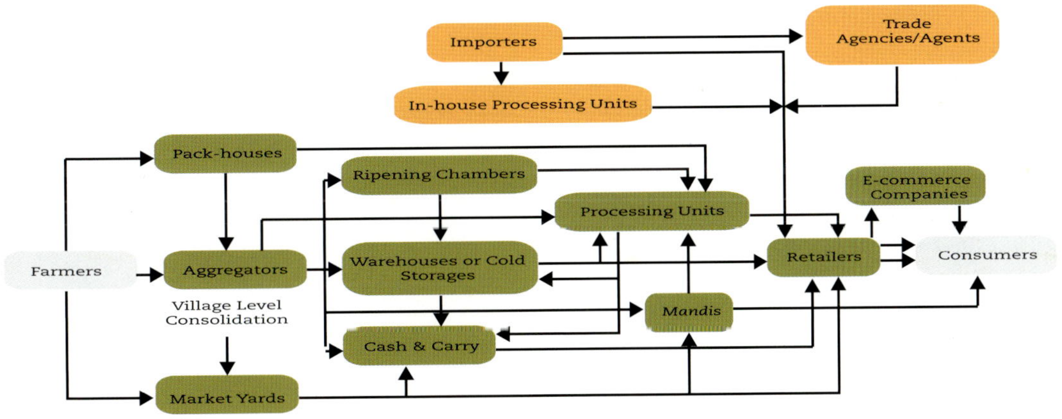

Source: Authors discussion with supply chain agents.

2.1 Production of Fruits and Vegetables

A large variety of fruits and vegetables are produced in India due to its varied climatic conditions. The country ranks second in the production of fruits and vegetables in the world, after China. Among fruits, the country is the largest producer of bananas, papayas and mangoes in the world, while among vegetables, it has the largest production base for okra and ginger. With a large and growing population and a diverse raw material base, India plays a pivotal role in the global demand and supply of food products (for details, see Food and Agriculture Organization (FAO), 2012).

During 2013-14, India produced 88.98 million metric tonnes of fruits and 162.89 million metric tonnes of vegetables. The year-on-year productivity of fruits and vegetables has remained more or less constant since the year 2004-05.

During 2013-14, India produced 88.98 million metric tonnes of fruits and 162.89 million metric tonnes of vegetables.[3] In the same period, the area under cultivation of fruits stood at 7.22 million hectares while vegetables were cultivated in 9.40 million hectares, which in aggregate is approximately 7 per cent of the total cropped area of the country.[4]

1. For details see *https://www.nabard.org/Publication/Rural_Pulse_final142014.pdf* (accessed on 1 December 2015).
2. Images Multimedia Private Limited (2015).
3. National Board of Horticulture, Government of India. Available at: *http://www.nhb.gov.in/area-pro/NHB_Database_2015.pdf* (accessed on 30 November 2015).
4. Department of Scientific and Industrial Research, Ministry of Science and Technology, Government of India. Available at *http://dsir.gov.in/reports/ittp_tedo/agro/AF_Farm_Fruits_Vegetables_Intro.pdf* (accessed on 30 November 2015).

Figure 2.2

Year-on-Year Productivity for Fruits and Vegetables from 2002-03 to 2013-14

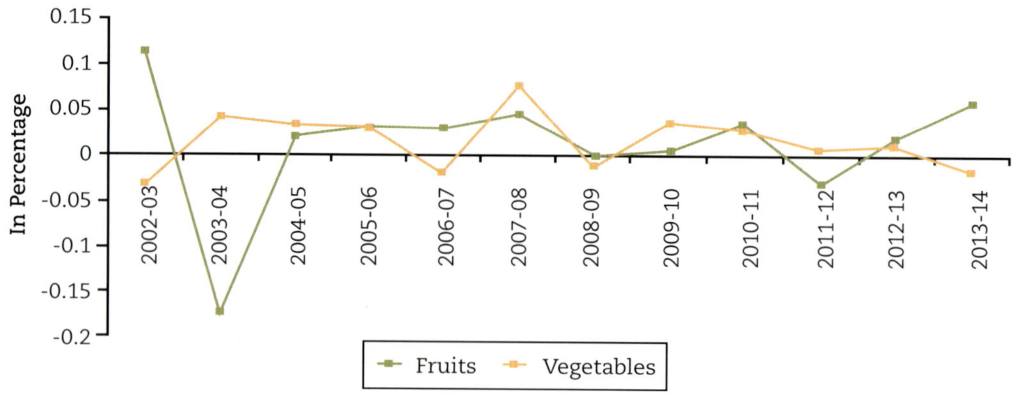

Source: Compiled from National Horticulture Board (2014), Page 2, Table titled: "Indian Horticulture Production at a Glance". Available at: *http://www.nhb.gov.in/area-pro/NHB_Database_2015.pdf* (accessed on 30 November 2015).

Figure 2.2 shows that the compound annual growth rate (CAGR) for fruit and vegetables productivity calculated for the period 2001-02 to 2013-14 is 0.012 and 0.016 respectively.[5] The statistics on production and area under cultivation for fruits and vegetables respectively, over the period 2001-02 to 2013-14 is given in Appendix A (Tables A.1 and A.2). The year-on-year productivity has remained more or less constant since 2004-05.

The major fruits and vegetables produced in India during 2013-14 are given in Figures 2.3 and 2.4 respectively and the top 10 states in production of fruits and vegetables are given in Figures 2.5 and 2.6 respectively.

Figure 2.3

Production Share of Major Fruits in India (2013-14)

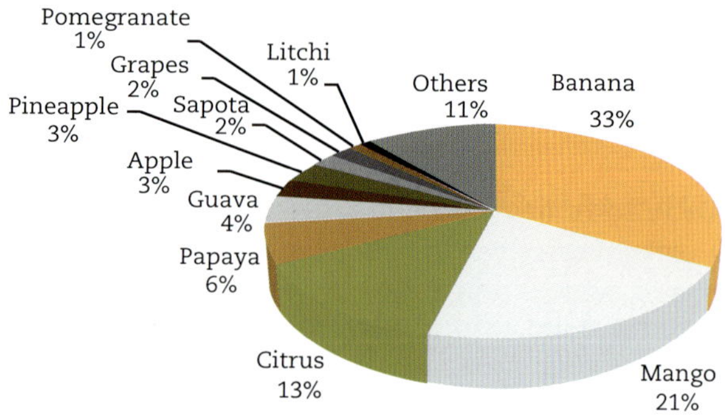

Source: Compiled from National Horticulture Board (2014), Page 4, Table titled: "Area and Production Estimates for Horticulture Crops." Available at: *http://www.nhb.gov.in/area-pro/NHB_Database_2015.pdf* (accessed on 30 November 2015).

There are variations in the production of fruits and vegetables across states.

Figure 2.4

Production of Major Vegetables in India (2013-14)

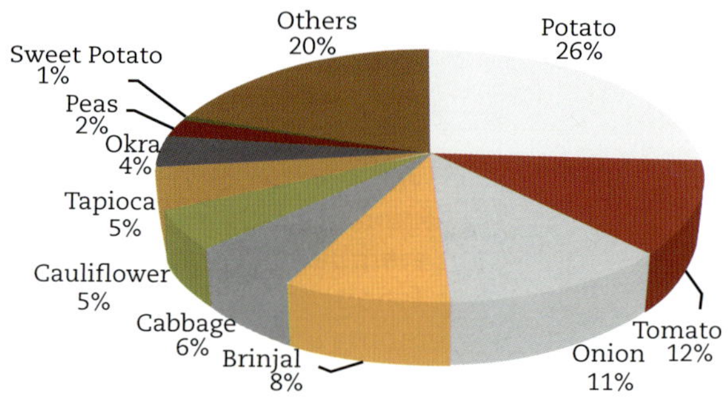

Source: Compiled from National Horticulture Board (2014), Page 4, Table titled: "Area and Production Estimates for Horticulture Crops." Available at: *http://www.nhb.gov.in/area-pro/NHB_Database_2015.pdf* (accessed on 30 November 2015).

Five states namely, Maharashtra, Andhra Pradesh, Gujarat, Tamil Nadu and Uttar Pradesh accounted for 52 per cent of total fruit production in 2013-14.

Overall, one can conclude that a wide variety of fruits and vegetables are produced in India, but the production varies across states, depending upon factors such as climatic conditions and soil type, among others. The analysis also highlights the fact

5. The CAGR calculates the change in productivity over the years, taking into account the effect of annual compounding.

West Bengal, Uttar Pradesh, Bihar, Madhya Pradesh and Gujarat accounted for 50 per cent of total vegetable production in 2013-14.

Figure 2.5

Top 10 States in Production of Fruits (2013-14)

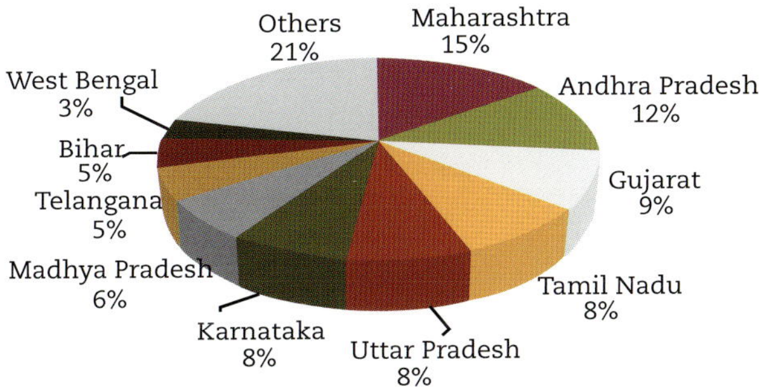

Note: This includes all states and union territories in India.

Source: Compiled from National Horticulture Board (2014), Page 8, Table titled: "State-wise Area, Production and Productivity of Fruits." Available at: *http://www.nhb.gov.in/area-pro/NHB_Database_2015.pdf* (accessed on 30 November 2015).

Figure 2.6

Top 10 States in Production of Vegetables (2013-14)

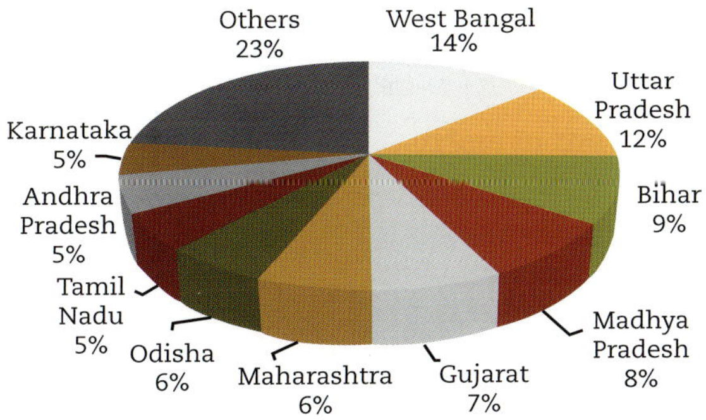

Note: This includes all states and union territories in India.

Source: Compiled from National Horticulture Board (2014), Page 10, Table titled: "State-wise Area, Production and Productivity of Vegetables." Available at: *http://www.nhb.gov.in/area-pro/NHB_Database_2015.pdf* (accessed on 30 November 2015).

that there has been very little improvement in the productivity of fruits and vegetables in the last decade. This is a cause for concern.

In a globalised world, production alone does not determine consumption. The consumption depends on other factors as well such as value addition, extent of wastage, extent of processing and trade. The next section focuses on trade in fruits and vegetables in India.

2.2 Trade in Fruits and Vegetables

Indian trade in agriculture, raw materials and processed food products has increased over time. This is also true for trade in fresh and processed fruits and vegetables. The vast production base in India offers opportunities for export of fruits and vegetables. Alongside, a large population with a growing middle and upper income group is generating demand for the import of food products in fresh and processed forms. Yet, the share of Indian exports and imports of fruits and vegetables in the world remains at a low of 2 per cent and 3 per cent respectively, as reported by United Nations (UN) Comtrade for the year 2013.[6]

India is a net importer of fruits and vegetables.

The Directorate General of Foreign Trade (DGFT) under the Ministry of Commerce and Industry provides data on trade in agricultural commodities in India.[7] In 2013-14, total exports of fruits and vegetables amounted to $2,979.36 million, while total imports were valued at $4,204.55 million.[8] The major share of India's exports of fruits and vegetables goes to the United Arab Emirates (UAE), the US, Pakistan and Bangladesh, while imports come largely from Canada, Myanmar, US and Australia. Among fruits, grapes and mangoes are major exports while dates and apples are major imports by value. Among vegetables, onions and tomatoes are major exports while dried leguminous vegetables such as peas and beans are major imports by value.

In the period 2001-02 to 2013-14, Indian exports of fruits and vegetables grew at a CAGR of 0.10 and 0.16

6. Source: UN Comtrade Database. Calculations have been made for the calendar year. Available at: *http://wits.worldbank.org/* (accessed on 30 November 2015).

7. In the listing provided by the DGFT, the category of vegetables includes all edible varieties along with certain roots and tubers such as potato, yam, etc. (coded 07 in the Indian Tariff Classification based on Harmonised System of Coding [ITC HS]) and the category of fruits includes all edible varieties of fruit and nut along with melons (coded 08 in ITC HS).

8. Data provided has been calculated for the financial year 2013-14.

Figure 2.7

Trade in Fruits in Metric Tonnes (2001-02 to 2013-14)

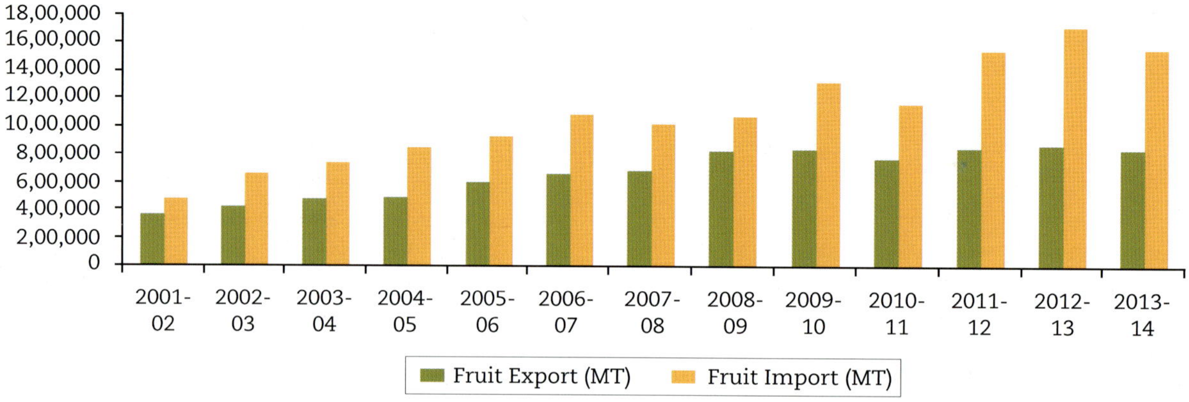

Source: Extracted from DGFT, Ministry of Commerce and Industry. Available at: *http://commerce.nic.in/eidb/default.asp* (accessed on 30 November 2015).

Figure 2.8

Trade in Vegetables in Metric Tonnes (2001-02 to 2013-14)

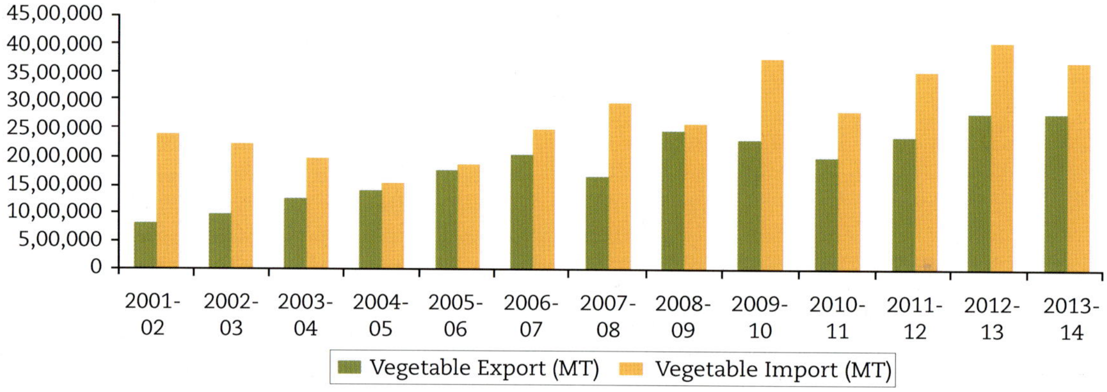

Source: Extracted from DGFT, Ministry of Commerce and Industry. Available at: *http://commerce.nic.in/eidb/default.asp* (accessed on 30 November 2015).

respectively by value while imports have risen at 0.19 and 0.10 respectively in value terms. In volume terms also, India's overall trade in fruits and vegetables has increased overtime. The import of fruits and vegetables is more than exports in terms of volume.

The gap between import and export is greater for fruits when compared to vegetables. Figures 2.7 and 2.8 show trade in fruit and vegetable volumes for India for the period 2001-02 to 2013-14.

Figures 2.7 and 2.8 show that in spite of a large and varied production base, India is a net importer of fruits and vegetables. In the case of fruits, the trade balance has become negative since the year 2008. In the past, India had imposed high tariffs on fruits and vegetables. However, as India entered into trade agreements, tariffs on some product categories have been liberalised under these agreements. Figure 2.9 highlights the treatment of fruits and vegetables under different trade agreements. It is important to note that fruits and vegetables that have a large domestic market (for example, bananas and mangoes among fruits) are generally in the sensitive lists or exclusion lists of India in its trade agreements. For

> Trade is rising and it is likely to grow further. At present, India has high tariffs on fruits and vegetables; however, as it has entered into trade agreements, tariffs on some product categories have been liberalised under these agreements. Therefore, it is likely that India's imports may rise in these categories and the trade balance will worsen.

Figure 2.9

Treatment of Fruits and Vegetables under Select Trade Agreements

Trade Agreement	Trading Partner(s)	Date of Signing	Date of Enforcement	Status of Agriculture and Food Processing
South Asia Free Trade Area (SAFTA)	Bangladesh, India, Nepal, Sri Lanka, Afghanistan, Bhutan, Maldives and Pakistan	January 2004	January 2006	A majority of the fresh and processed fruits and vegetables (including fresh, dried, frozen, canned and preserved forms) are in the sensitive list. Also referred to as the negative list in the SAFTA, these products are excluded from any duty reduction or elimination.
India-ASEAN Free Trade Agreement (FTA)	India, Brunei Darussalam, Cambodia, Indonesia, Lao People's Democratic Republic, Malaysia, Myanmar, Philippines, Singapore, Thailand and Vietnam	August 2009	January 2010	A majority of the fresh and processed fruits and vegetables (including fresh and dried forms) are excluded from the FTA. Other products are classified under Normal Track 1 where duties were reduced to zero by December 2013. These include fruits and nuts, uncooked or cooked by steaming or boiling in water, frozen, whether or not containing added sugar or other sweetening matter, frozen fruits, etc. Products like apples fall under Normal Track 2 under which the duty is to be reduced to zero by December 2016. There are several spices like cloves, etc., that are in the sensitive list under which any duty above 5 per cent is to be reduced to 5 per cent by 2019.
India-Singapore Comprehensive Economic Cooperation Agreement (CECA)	India and Singapore	June 2005	August 2008	A majority of fresh and preserved fruits and vegetables are excluded from the list.
India-Korea Comprehensive Economic Partnership Agreement (CEPA)	India and Korea	August 2009	January 2010	A majority of fresh and processed fruits and vegetables are either in the 'excluded' or 'sensitive' list. Those in the excluded list are excluded from any tariff concessions. These include pineapples, apples, plums, figs and dates, among others. Those in the sensitive list such as mangoes (fresh and processed), guavas and oranges (fresh and dried) will have reduction in duty by 50 per cent of the base rate in ten equal annual stages beginning on the date this agreement enters into force, and such goods shall remain at 50 per cent of the base rate, effective January 1 of year nine.
India-Malaysia CECA	India and Malaysia	February 2011	July 2011	The tariff schedule with Malaysia is similar to the India-ASEAN FTA schedule.
India-Japan CEPA	India and Japan	February 2011	August 2011	A number of commodities such as peas, beans, onions etc. are excluded from the trade agreement while others such as asparagus, spinach, etc., fall under the B10 category, where the duty has to be reduced in 11 equal instalments—from the base rate to free.

Source: Compiled from the Tariff Schedule of India in different Trade Agreements. Accessible at: Department of Commerce, Government of India. *http://commerce.nic.in/MOC/index.asp* (accessed on 30 November 2015).

example, in the India-Korea CEPA that came into force in January 2010, mango (fresh and processed) and guava are listed as sensitive commodities, with a reduction in duty by 50 per cent of the base rate expected in 10 annual stages. Since most of India's existing trade agreements have a phased out tariff plan, the impact on trade in fruits and vegetables will be seen after 2016 in most cases.[9]

Figure 2.9 presents the status of the food processing sector and the agriculture sector in India's current trade agreements. Overall, India tries to restrict imports of fruits and vegetables through high tariffs and by putting them in the sensitive list for trade agreements. However, through trade agreements, tariffs in select fruits and vegetables are likely to come down in a phased manner.

As India enters into more trade agreements, especially with countries such as Australia and New Zealand and regions such as the European Union (EU), that have a strong interest in liberalising agricultural trade, it is expected that trade in fruits and vegetables will increase. This will necessarily provide Indian consumers access to a wider variety of fruits and vegetables. On the other hand, India's ability to increase exports will depend on the quality of the produce, global competitiveness of production, etc.

There have been changes in the patterns of production, exports and imports across different fruits and vegetables over time. Tables A.3 and A.4 provided in Appendix A map this change for select fruits (banana and mango) and vegetables (onion and tomato) for the period 2001-02 to 2013-14.

2.3 Consumption of Fruits and Vegetables

It is extremely difficult to get data on net availability of fruits and vegetables for consumption. This is because net availability is broadly calculated as the sum of total production and imports minus wastage and exports. The disaggregated data for wastage of different fruits and vegetable is not available. Some organisations have tried to estimate wastage but the numbers vary.[10]

9. For details, see the Tariff Schedule of India in Different Trade Agreements. Accessible at: Department of Commerce, Government of India. *http://commerce.nic.in/MOC/index.asp* (accessed on 30 November 2015).

10. For example, see Central Institute of Post Harvest Engineering & Technology (CIPHET) 2013 and Planning Commission (2012).

> Between 1993 and 2011, the proportion of household expenditure on total food items has decreased in both rural and urban households. However, the proportion of income spent on fruits and vegetables has not changed much over time.

The NSSO under the Ministry of Statistics and Programme Implementation conducts surveys to collect information on household consumer expenditure at the national and state level. The rural and urban sector lists as provided by the Census is taken as the survey frame for each round of the survey, covering the entire geographical area of the country using the random sampling technique.

Figures 2.10 and 2.11 highlight the monthly per capita expenditure (MPCE) on vegetables, fruits and total food items as a proportion of total monthly expenditure for rural and urban households, respectively. This information is provided for certain points over the period from 1993-94 to 2011-12. It must be mentioned that each report reviewed is based on surveys that gather expenditure patterns across the country for the duration of a year, thereby accounting for any seasonal variation in availability and consumption of food items.

It can be seen from these figures that over the period 1993 to 2011, the proportion of household expenditure on total food items has decreased in both rural and urban households. However, the proportions of income spent on fruits and vegetables for rural and urban households have not changed much over time. This can be due to an absolute increase in quantity purchased or an increase in the prices of fruits and vegetables over time or a combination of both.

Tables 2.1 and 2.2 highlight the change in the consumption patterns of select fruits, vegetables and spices in the country over the period 2009-10 to 2011-12 for rural and urban households, respectively. The fruits and vegetables have been grouped according to FAO (2015).

From the Tables 2.1 and 2.2, it can be inferred that during the time period 2009-10 to 2011-12, for rural households, monthly per capita consumption increased by 13 per cent, while per capita expenditure rose by 43 per cent for the listed fruits, vegetables and spices. Likewise, for urban households, per

Figure 2.10

Monthly Per Capita Expenditure in Rural Households—All India

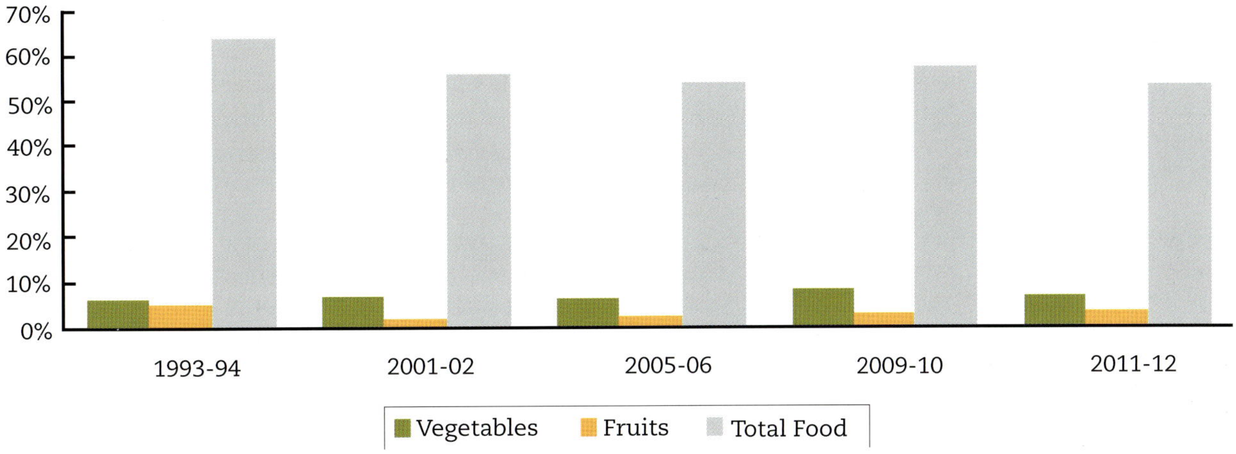

Note: Total food includes cereals, pulses, milk and dairy products, oil, egg and meat, fruits and vegetables, sugar, salt and spices and beverages, refreshments and procured (including purchased cooked meals) food items. Time period of the survey is from the month of July of the previous year to June next year.

Source: Compiled from various NSSO (50th, 57th, 62nd, 66th and 68th) Round reports.

Figure 2.11

Monthly Per Capita Expenditure in Urban Households—All India

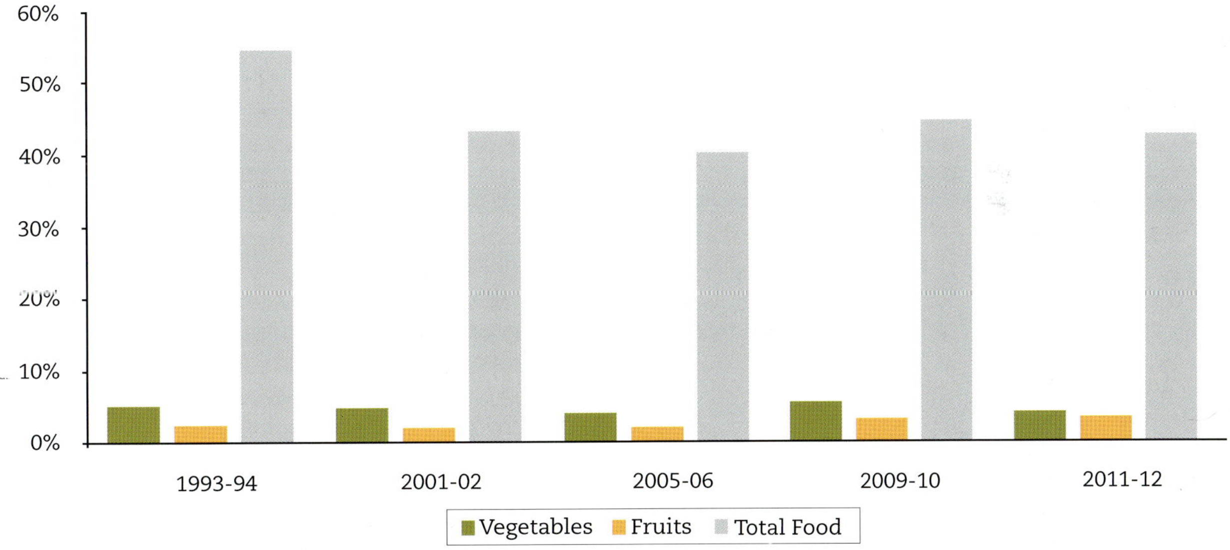

Note: Total food includes cereals, pulses, milk and dairy products, oil, egg and meat, fruits and vegetables, sugar, salt and spices and beverages, refreshments and procured (including purchased cooked meals) food items. Time period of the survey is from the month of July of the previous year to June next year.

Source: Compiled from various NSSO (50th, 57th, 62nd, 66th and 68th) Round reports.

Table 2.1

Monthly Consumption Patterns for Select Fruits, Vegetables and Spices in Rural India

Rural		*2009-10*			*2011-12*		
FAO Group	*Food Group*	*Per Capita Consumption (Kg)*	*Per Capita Consumption (INR)*	*% of Consuming Households*	*Per Capita Consumption (Kg)*	*Per Capita Consumption (INR)*	*% of Consuming Households*
Fruiting Vegetables (Including Melons)	Tomatoes	0.537	7.47	71.8	0.586	9.24	74.6
	Eggplant	0.518	6.42	64.3	0.428	6.73	57.8
	Okra	0.202	3.13	32.8	0.209	4.32	33.6
	Parval/Patal	0.097	1.42	12.7	0.105	2.14	15.5
	Pumpkin	0.25	2.21	24.8	0.359	4.37	33.2
	Green Chilli	0.145	4.09	81.6	0.152	4.94	83.1
Brassica Vegetables	Cabbages	0.275	2.9	31.4	0.227	2.88	27.6
	Cauliflower	0.302	3.53	28.6	0.284	3.95	28.4
Leafy Vegetables	Spinach, Others	0.605	5.84	58.7	0.59	7.65	61.2
Root, Bulb or Tuberous Vegetables	Onion	0.741	10.89	94.9	0.842	11.39	95.9
	Garlic (Gm)	75.253	5	87.9	74.142	5.51	89.6
	Carrot	0.073	1.08	12.4	0.078	1.34	12.8
	Radish	0.186	1.43	19.6	0.147	1.38	17.2
Tropical and Sub-tropical Fruits	Banana (No.)	3.861	5.88	34.4	4.181	8.12	36.5
	Pineapple (No.)	0.012	0.12	0.8	0.012	0.17	0.7
	Guavas	0.07	1	8.3	0.088	1.44	9.1
	Mango	0.108	2.54	7.5	0.16	4.79	10.4
	Papaya	0.027	0.38	2.5	0.053	0.91	4
Citrus Fruits	Orange, *Mausambi* (No.)	0.364	1.05	4.9	0.401	1.51	5.3
	Lemon (No.)	1.274	1.19	21.6	1.211	1.88	29
Pome and Stone Fruits	Apple	0.045	2.73	6.1	0.058	4.74	8
	Pears/*Nashpati*	0.003	0.07	0.3	0.002	0.05	0.2
Melons	Water Melons	0.072	0.58	2.9	0.081	0.81	3.3
	Kharbooza	0.023	0.21	1.2	0.025	0.33	1.3
Berries	Grapes	0.026	1.23	5.4	0.038	1.97	7.3
	Berries	0.005	0.07	0.8	0.006	0.09	0.8
	Litchi	0.002	0.06	0.2	0.003	0.18	0.5
Spices	Ginger (Gm)	42.709	2.76	58.9	57.142	3.28	6.94
	Turmeric (Gm)	50.507	5.95	93.5	46.637	7.6	94.9

Note: Time period of the survey is from the month of July of the previous year to June next year.

Source: National Sample Survey (NSS) Report No. 541 (66/1.0/3) and NSS Report No. 558 (68/1.0/2). Available at *http://mail.mospi.gov.in/index.php/home*. (accessed on 25 July 2015).

capita consumption increased by 7 per cent, while per capita expenditure rose by 26 per cent for the fruits, vegetables and spices listed. In both rural and urban settings, the number of households reporting consumption of the particular food items had increased marginally. Therefore, it may be concluded that while consumption of fruits and vegetables has broadly increased among rural and urban households, inflation in prices of food items has played a major role in raising household expenditure.

In recent years, there has been significant inflation in food prices. Therefore, consumption has to be measured taking into account both quantity consumed and prices. The next section will focus on price movements in the fruit and vegetable sector in India.

Table 2.2

Monthly Consumption Patterns for Select Fruits, Vegetables and Spices in Urban India

Urban		*2009-10*			*2011-12*		
FAO Group	*Food Group*	*Per Capita Consumption (Kg)*	*Per Capita Consumption (INR)*	*% of Consuming Households*	*Per Capita Consumption (Kg)*	*Per Capita Consumption (INR)*	*% of Consuming Households*
Fruiting Vegetables (Including Melons)	Tomatoes	0.757	11.66	81.6	0.806	13.9	84.8
	Eggplants	0.441	6.86	61.1	0.358	6.96	53.8
	Okra	0.282	5.86	45	0.281	7.46	44.3
	Parval/Patal	0.087	1.68	11.9	0.106	2.65	16.1
	Pumpkin	0.166	1.89	19.9	0.281	4.44	28.8
	Green Chilly	0.148	4.42	79.6	0.166	5.69	81.4
Brassica Vegetables	Cabbages	0.337	4.6	41.4	0.271	4.61	36
	Cauliflower	0.362	5.92	37.7	0.326	6.5	36
Leafy Vegetables	Spinach, Others	0.497	6.76	56.3	0.528	9.74	59
Root, Bulb or Tuberous Vegetables	Onion	0.854	13.34	90.3	0.951	13.66	90.8
	Garlic (Gm)	83.356	6.08	83.3	81.097	6.52	84.3
	Carrot	0.153	2.77	25.9	0.153	3.26	25.4
	Radish	0.176	1.79	21.1	0.14	1.73	17.6
Tropical and Sub-tropical Fruits	Banana (No.)	6.647	12.18	52.2	6.694	15.31	53.2
	Pineapple (No.)	0.025	0.41	1.4	0.027	0.5	1.3
	Guavas	0.087	1.62	9.9	0.091	1.9	9.7
	Mango	0.158	5.52	10.9	0.202	8.33	13.4
	Papaya	0.079	1.55	5.9	0.081	1.76	6.1
Citrus Fruits	Orange, *Mausambi* (No.)	0.86	3.2	10.3	1.021	4.48	12.4
	Lemon (No.)	1.72	3	36.9	2.117	3.72	43.8
Pome and Stone Fruits	Apple	0.158	12.09	19.4	0.191	18.1	22.7
	Pears/*Nashpati*	0.006	0.23	0.8	0.004	0.2	0.5
Melons	Water Melons	0.094	1.05	3.9	0.094	1.34	4
	Kharbooza	0.032	0.57	1.9	0.025	0.46	1.4
Berries	Grapes	0.073	3.51	11.3	0.084	4.84	13
	Berries	0.004	0.08	0.5	0.003	0.09	0.5
	Litchi	0.004	0.25	0.7	0.008	0.48	0.9
Spices	Ginger (Gm)	60.644	4.06	68.1	73.318	4.34	76.8
	Turmeric (Gm)	49.985	6.26	87.7	46.349	8.32	89.5

Note: Time period of the survey is from the month of July of the previous year to June next year.

Source: NSS Report No. 541 (66/1.0/3) and NSS Report No. 558 (68/1.0/2). Available at *http://mail.mospi.gov.in/index.php/home* (accessed on 25 July 2015).

2.4 Prices of Fruits and Vegetables

Prices of raw and processed agriculture products depend on production (including seasonality of production) of the food items, distance of the consumption point from production centres, cost of transportation and logistics, wastage, government policies (such as inter-state restrictions on movement of commodities or restrictions on imports), and taxes and duties in case of processed food items. Over the years, there has been significant food inflation across India.[11] Both demand and supply side factors have contributed to this surge in the prices of food commodities in the country. The total production of

11. See Bhattacharya and Sengupta (2015) and Eapen and Nair (2012).

Table 2.3

WPI for Select Fruits, Vegetables and Spices—All India (2005-2014)

FAO Group	*Food Group*	2005-06	2006-07	2007-08	2008-09	2009-10	2010-11	2011-12	2012-13	2013-14	2014-15
Fruiting Vegetables (Including Melons)	Tomatoes	119.05	125.56	123.82	153.24	153.56	190.39	184.39	172.30	307.38	314.17
	Eggplant	114.31	116.43	130.53	142.75	139.13	164.66	170.97	186.18	235.85	216.42
	Okra	102.68	115.24	123.33	133.84	145.53	174.80	237.15	232.56	252.18	221.92
Brassica Vegetables	Cabbage	127.32	119.51	157.11	168.51	150.65	214.58	211.59	271.96	336.38	315.54
	Cauliflower	101.32	97.45	101.45	125.52	124.38	169.87	145.93	153.00	174.68	191.80
Root, Bulb or Tuberous Vegetables	Onion	126.62	115.90	174.68	177.75	204.30	259.60	186.67	232.51	482.22	333.67
	Garlic	92.77	202.27	211.47	132.02	228.07	410.12	281.12	110.87	194.71	266.27
Tropical and Sub-tropical Fruits	Banana	110.57	115.28	120.56	132.45	146.62	163.01	173.42	210.53	246.64	288.22
	Pineapple	94.25	97.89	116.28	128.82	154.43	177.92	193.45	233.43	255.82	255.20
	Guava	119.92	121.32	120.38	125.20	110.43	177.67	148.32	99.83	156.28	302.97
	Mango	95.03	101.93	110.40	151.65	141.97	191.52	237.15	219.68	191.47	226.60
	Papaya	92.08	94.97	110.14	137.11	154.80	189.62	186.97	139.67	164.60	145.76
	Sapota	101.28	100.43	124.07	116.20	149.04	174.02	209.45	232.81	232.18	238.21
Citrus Fruits	Orange	113.30	123.23	113.49	138.25	148.63	185.32	237.35	228.29	208.85	237.72
	Lemon	131.73	165.05	194.99	183.42	164.70	197.49	236.16	216.85	191.97	260.17
Pome and Stone Fruits	Apple	100.88	124.79	124.62	134.74	171.23	173.59	220.38	241.42	228.61	240.10
Berries	Grapes	98.72	109.85	126.48	127.17	124.78	188.85	221.20	195.87	212.00	251.88
	Litchi	-	-	79.70	77.10	102.70	179.20	119.70	153.00	160.40	204.40
Spices	Ginger (Fresh)	70.39	44.18	57.72	98.22	106.65	114.54	79.98	83.21	200.97	213.11
	Turmeric	90.45	88.14	82.77	105.42	210.32	401.72	214.87	166.32	215.28	229.58

Source: Office of the Economic Adviser, Ministry of Commerce and Industry Available at: *http://www.eaindustry.nic.in/home.asp* (accessed on 8 December 2015)

fruits and vegetables in India has not been successful in keeping up with increased demand. Lack of rainfall and natural disasters such as floods can lead to an increase in prices. Additional factors such as restrictions on imports, hoarding and a fragmented supply chain have also propelled inflation (see Mukherjee et al., 2014).

> Inflation in prices of food items has played a major role in raising household expenditure. Further, there are inter-state differences in the prices of fruits and vegetables in India—this often affects the consumption patterns.

The Office of the Economic Adviser, under the Ministry of Commerce and Industry, publishes data on the wholesale price index (WPI) on a weekly basis, which shows that the prices of fruits and vegetables have increased over the last few years. Figure 2.12 plots the change in wholesale price indices of fruits and vegetables for the period 2005-06 to 2014-15.

Table 2.3 provides the WPI for select fruits, vegetables and spices sold across the country over the period of 2005-06 to 2014-15. The fruits and vegetables have been grouped according to FAO (2015). It can be inferred from the tables above that the price level for the category of fruits and vegetables has risen significantly over the period.

In India, the prices of fruits and vegetables vary widely across cities, towns and rural areas within each state and even across different markets in the same state (see Tables B.1 to B.7 in Appendix B for select fruits and vegetables). A careful analysis of the available data shows that variations exist across city centres inspected and time periods of sale. For example, wholesale average price of cauliflower rises in the summer month of July and declines by almost 92 per cent in January in Delhi in 2014 (see Figure 2.13). In the case of orange, while Mumbai had availability of the fruit throughout the year, the average price was also lower here than in other cities. In other cases of major fruits such as banana and vegetables such as onion, price variations were smaller through the year. However, inter-state variations can be inferred from the price differences observed across cities, leading to differences in the consumption patterns.

Figure 2.12

WPI for Fruits and Vegetables—All India (2005-06 to 2014-15)

Note: Data is provided for financial years, with base as 2004-05= 100.

Source: Office of the Economic Adviser, Ministry of Commerce and Industry; Available at: *http://www.eaindustry.nic.in/home.asp* (accessed on 8 December 2015).

Figure 2.13

Price Movement of Cauliflower and Okra in Delhi (2014) (in INR per Quintal)

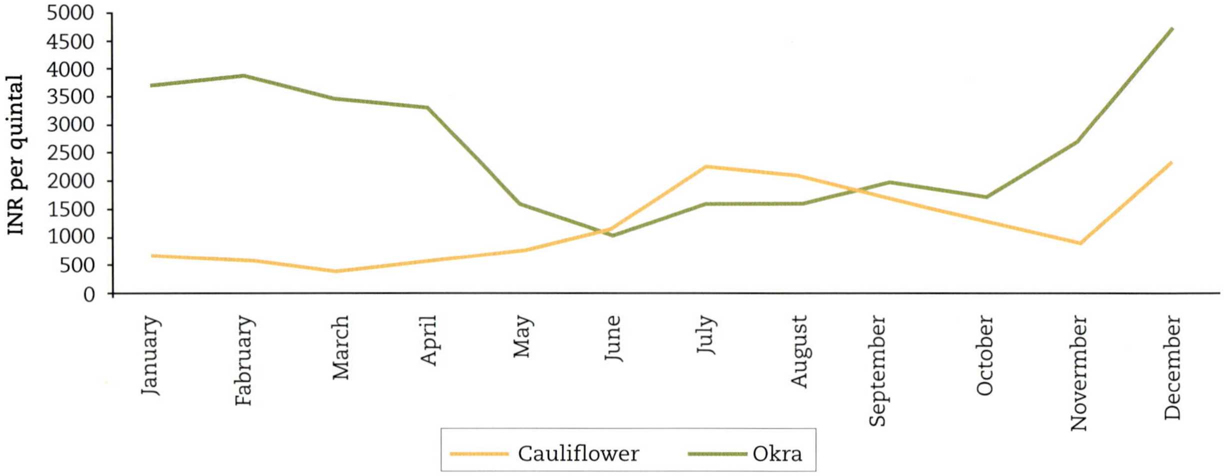

Source: Extracted from the NHB website *http://nhb.gov.in/OnlineClient/MonthwiseAnnualPriceandArrivalReport.aspx?enc=3ZOO8K5CzcdC/Yq6HcdlxJ4o5jmAcGG5Q GUXX3BIAP4=* (accessed on 30 November 2015).

The above analysis highlights that there is a gap in the production and consumption of fruits and vegetables in India. While India is one of the largest producers of several fruits and vegetables, it is also a net importer of fruits and vegetables. The gap between the supply and demand for fruits and vegetables is one of the reasons for rise in prices and variations in prices across products and states. The available secondary information shows that there are several bottlenecks throughout the supply chain from the farm to the fork, leading to inefficiencies. It is, therefore, important to understand the policy framework applicable to the fruits and vegetables supply chain in India. Domestic regulations affect the production and distribution of fruits and vegetables in a country. The next section discusses some of the applicable regulations affecting the supply and consumption of fruits and vegetables in India.

3

Regulations Affecting the Supply and Consumption of Fruits and Vegetables

Government policy can play a key role in increasing the production of fruits and vegetables, price stabilisation, streamlining of the supply chain, ensuring steady supply of products, creating awareness among consumers about the benefits of consuming fruits and vegetables, and ensuring food safety and standards. Due to the quasi-federal governance structure in India, multiple government agencies are involved in the food supply chain. Agriculture and retail are under the jurisdiction of the state government. The states do play a significant role in decisions on product sourcing, taxes and inter-state mobility of agricultural products. The central government gives broad guidelines and strategies for the agricultural supply chain, but implementation is largely at the discretion of the state governments.

Both the central and state governments give priority to the agriculture sector and there is a policy focus on the production of fruits and vegetables. To promote horticulture, the central government launched the National Horticulture Mission in 2005-06, in partnership with the states. Several schemes have been launched for incentivising the sector. For instance, the Mega Food Park Scheme of the Ministry of Food Processing Industries focus on the storage, ripening and processing of fruits and vegetables. Agriculture also receives fertiliser subsidies and is exempt from direct taxes and electricity charges. In addition, several incentives, tax concessions and grants are given by different departments of the central government and by states to promote cold storage development and the establishment of a food supply chain.

The food supply chain is a highly regulated sector in India. Regulations are imposed by the central and state governments to protect small farmers, manufacturers and retailers and to ensure food safety and quality. One of the key regulations related to sourcing is the Agriculture Produce and Marketing Committee (APMC) Act. The Act requires that all agriculture products should be sold in government-regulated markets (called *mandis*). Under this Act, retailers and manufacturers were previously restricted from entering into contract manufacturing or sourcing directly from farmers. This Act has been changed in some states such as Karnataka, which now allows direct sourcing and contract manufacturing but there are states such as West Bengal, which still do not allow contract manufacturing. Restrictive trade practices are governed by the Competition Act, 2002, which was amended in 2007 and this is also applicable to the food supply chain.

There are restrictions on foreign investment in segments of the food supply chain. For example, only 51 per cent foreign direct investment (FDI) is allowed in multi-brand retail subject to certain conditions. In certain other areas of the food supply chain, such as manufacturing, food processing and cold chain development, the government has not only allowed 100 per cent FDI but both the central and state governments offer tax holidays, subsidies, grants and other incentives. More recently, in November 2015, the government tried to liberalise and streamline the FDI policy and some of it can impact the food supply chain positively. For example, 100 per cent FDI is allowed in horticulture, cultivation of vegetables and mushrooms, development and production of seeds and plantation material and services related to agro and allied sectors through the automatic route.[1] A manufacturer will now be permitted to sell his/her product through wholesale and/or retail, including through e-commerce through the automatic route. Further, 100 per cent FDI is allowed for e-commerce to undertake business-to-business (B2B) operations and single-brand retail trading and 100 per cent FDI is now permitted under the automatic route in duty free shops located and operated in the customs bonded areas such as Special Economic Zones (SEZs). Along with these, the government has eased exit norms and the lock-in period for construction, which may encourage foreign investment in supply chain infrastructure. Thus, overall, there is a strong policy push to attract FDI in all segments of the supply chain except food and grocery retailing.

Imports play a key role in enhancing consumers' access to fruits and vegetables and in price stabilisation. The Export Inspection Council (EIC) along with the Ministry of Commerce and Industry has laid down guidelines and regulations for imported commodities. These are based on international standards—Codex Alimentarius. The EIC monitors imports of food items and checks the condition of the hold in which goods are transported, the visual/physical appearance of the goods and labelling of the products. The port health officer checks the samples of imported food products. In addition, every imported food item is examined at the time of its import to ensure that it has a valid shelf life of not less than 60 per cent of its original shelf

1. In India, FDI is allowed through two routes: (a) automatic route and (b) government route. Under the automatic route, no prior approval of the government is required, while under the government route, proposals for FDI have to be cleared by the Foreign Investment Promotion Board (FIPB), constituted by the Ministry of Finance.

life;[2] food articles that do not meet this condition cannot be sold in the domestic market.

In India, imports of fruits and vegetables are restricted by high tariffs as compared to other developing countries such as Thailand. Further, India is defensive about opening up trade in agricultural products under trade agreements and the country does impose certain sanitary and phytosanitary (SPS) measures and technical barriers to trade (TBT) primarily to ensure food safety and quality, which can restrict imports.

Ensuring food safety is a key component of any government policy and India is no exception. India has enacted the Food Safety and Standards Act (FSSA), 2006, the implementation of which is compulsory across all states. This Act led to the establishment of the Food Safety and Standards Authority of India (FSSAI) that lays down safety and quality standards for food items and regulates their manufacture, storage, packaging, labelling, distribution, sale and import. This Act applies to the entire supply chain, except farmers and, therefore, does not cover food safety related to issues resulting from the use of pesticide or other farm practices.

All food business operators in India, whether domestic or foreign, require an FSSAI licence to conduct business in the country. The FSSAI issues guidelines on use of ingredients, licensing and registration, how product packaging and labelling has to be done, etc.,[3] it also sets food product standards. India is gradually aligning its food safety standards to the Codex Alimentarius, which are laid down by the FAO of the UN under a joint WHO/FAO Programme. In 2013, the National Codex Contact Point (NCCP) for India was established under the FSSAI. With the development of new products, the FSSAI keeps releasing advisories and draft regulations to accommodate the dynamism of the product space. For example, the FSSAI released the Draft Food Safety and Standards (*Food or Health Supplements, Nutraceuticals, Foods for Special Dietary Uses, Foods for Special Medical Purpose, Functional Foods, and Novel Food*) Regulations, 2015.[4] This draft specifies the definitions, criteria, packaging and labelling requirements, etc., required for food supplements/nutraceuticals.

While these are largely regulations applicable to backward linkages in the fruits and vegetables supply chain, there are several regulations applicable to front-end operations. The key regulation for the store-based retail format is the Shops and Establishment Act, which regulates working conditions and shop opening timings. This Act varies across states. Further, a food and grocery retailer has to take clearances from about 50 authorities from different departments of the government including police, environment, fire and labour. With evolving retail formats, the government is in the process of designing regulations for non-store retail formats such as e-commerce and direct selling.

To ensure that the consumer gets products of the right quality and quantity, the Legal Metrology Act, 2009, establishes uniform standards of weights and measures. According to the Legal Metrology Packaged Commodities Rules, 2011, (which came into force on April 1, 2011), manufacturing, packaging, selling or importing any pre-packaged commodity is prohibited unless it is in a standard quantity and carries all prescribed declarations. This Act requires that the maximum retail price should be mentioned on the product label to protect consumer interest.

The key regulation for consumer protection is the Consumer Protection Act, 1986, and the Consumer Protection (Amendment) Act, 2002. The Ministry of Consumer Affairs is the nodal agency for this regulation, which has provisions for the establishment of consumer councils and similar authorities to settle consumer grievances and disputes.

While the available secondary information broadly gives the production and consumption situation in India, it does not provide information on the detailed consumption patterns, consumer perspective, factors determining the consumption patterns and awareness about regulations. To fill this lacuna, a primary survey was conducted and the results are summarised in the following section.

---

2. *http://www.sethassociates.com/food-and-drug-industry-in-india.html* (accessed on 30 November 2015).
3. For details, see the Food Safety and Standards (Packaging and Labelling) Regulations, 2011. Available at *http://www.fssai.gov.in/Portals/0/Pdf/Food%20Safety%20and%20standards%20(Packaging%20and%20Labelling)%20regulation,%202011.pdf* (accessed on 26 November 2015).
4. For details, see *http://www.fssai.gov.in/Portals/0/Pdf/Draft_Notification_Food_Suppliment.pdf* (accessed on 27 November 2015).

4

Consumption of Fruits and Vegetables: The Primary Survey of Consumers

While the available secondary information broadly gives the production and consumption situation in India, it does not provide information on the detailed consumption patterns, consumer perspective, factors determining the consumption patterns and awareness about regulations. To fill this lacuna, a primary survey was conducted.

Most existing studies on the importance of fruits and vegetables in diet are based on health surveys. However, health surveys do not reflect purchase and consumption patterns thoroughly. The NSSO (2014) found that fruits and vegetables constitute a very small proportion of daily diet. In this section, we present a survey of consumers in India to delve more deeply into their consumption patterns. The purpose of the consumer survey is to find out: (a) the consumption patterns of fruits and vegetables, (b) consumers' awareness of nutritional content and chemical content in fruits and vegetables produced in India, (c) possible reasons for the shortfall in consumption wherever they exist, and (d) their expectation from the government. This section analyses the findings of the survey while the recommendations for the government are discussed in section 6.

The purpose of the consumer survey is to find out: (a) the consumption patterns of fruits and vegetables, (b) consumers' awareness of nutritional content and chemical content in fruits and vegetables produced in India, (c) possible reasons for the shortfall in consumption wherever they exist, and (d) their expectation from the government.

The survey covered 1,001 individuals drawn from households across 5 metro cities, namely National Capital Region (NCR) (New Delhi, Delhi; Gurgaon, Haryana; and Noida, Uttar Pradesh), Mumbai (Maharashtra), Chennai (Tamil Nadu), Hyderabad (Telangana) and Kolkata (West Bengal). A stratified random sample was chosen and trained investigators conducted face-to-face interviews using the recall methodology. The sample consisted of individuals from upper and middle income groups, which was further segregated according to the: (a) age group: respondents selected were 18 years or above in age, (b) sex: male or female, (c) socio-economic classification (SEC) category A and B[1] (d) occupation, (e) income level of the individual and the household, and (e) place of residence within the city (or pin code). Additional information about household composition was also gathered for stratification.

A semi-structured questionnaire was designed for the survey, which is enclosed in Appendix C. As can be seen from the questionnaire, respondents were asked about their purchases and intake of fruits and vegetables. Regarding information on intake of fruits and vegetables, the survey used a show card to demonstrate the serving size. Respondents were asked to answer questions related to the frequency of intake (days per week) and portion size of intake on a typical day (number of servings). Additionally, information on purchase of common fruits and vegetables from an identified list was collected to observe the pattern of regional variation, if any, across states. Respondents were asked to report their source of purchase (such as, online purchase, retail store, street vendor or wholesale market) to assess the most accessible distribution network. Information was also collected from them on the criteria on which their purchase was made and their preferences, e.g., organic *versus* inorganic, or branded *versus* unbranded. The respondents were asked questions to examine the possible reasons for the shortfall in intake of the desired quantity of fruits and vegetables, if any, as specified by the WHO.

The survey also collected information on consumer health and awareness. Respondents were questioned on their awareness of: (a) the beneficial effects of fruits and vegetables consumption and (b) regulations on food safety and consumer protection. Respondents were asked to mention current intake of food supplements, if any, along with their awareness of other brands of food supplements available, and their preferred mode of distribution of those products.

In total, 200 completely filled in interviews were conducted in each of the cities in the NCR, Kolkata, Chennai and Hyderabad and 201 interviews were conducted in Mumbai. The sample distribution is presented in Appendix D (Figures D.1 to D.4).

4.1 Composition of the Sample

Out of the 1,001 respondents, 578 are males (57.7 per cent) and the rest females. The age-group distribution of the sample is given in Table 4.1.

1. A SEC category can be determined with a combination of factors such as occupation, education level, ownership of consumer durables, etc.

Figure 4.1

Distribution of the Respondents by Annual Household Income Category (in numbers)

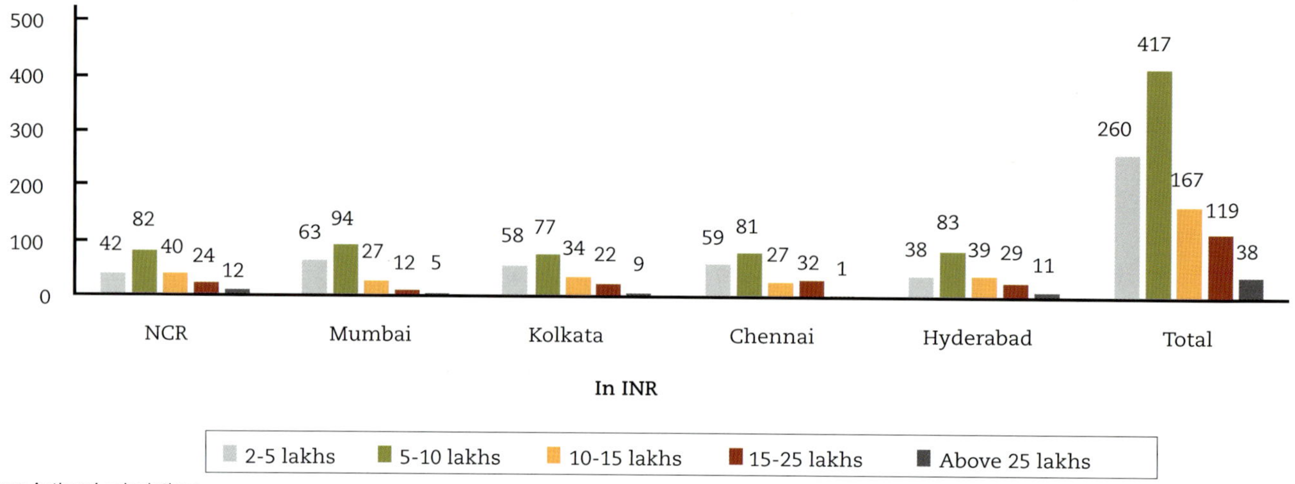

Source: Authors' calculations.

Table 4.1

Distribution of Sample by Age Groups

Age Group (in years)	*Number of Respondents*
18–25	113
25–35	300
35–50	382
50–60	158
>60	48
Total	1,001

Source: Authors' calculations.

Around 70 per cent of the sample has completed their graduation or even higher education; this is not surprising given that our sample is drawn from upper and middle income households across metro cities in India (see Figure D.1 in Appendix D). Respondents were asked to report their occupation and it has a wide range of variation ranging from officers to clerks and petty traders as well as students and housewives (see Figure D.2 in Appendix D).

The consumption and expenditure on fruits and vegetables can depend on the number of members in the family, number of earning members in the family and whether the person is staying away from home. The average number of members in a family in the sample is 4.5 while the average number of earning members in the family is 1.6. There is some variation across cities and Figure D.3 in Appendix D provides the average number of members and average number of earning members by different metro cities. Out of 1,001 respondents, 640 (63.9 per cent) belong to a nuclear family while 318 are from joint families (31.8 per cent) and a meagre 43 are single member families (4.3 per cent). Figure D.4 depicts the distribution of household composition city-wise in Appendix D. Last but not least, one of the primary determinants that can have a huge impact on the consumption patterns is household income. Figure 4.1 shows the distribution of the sample by income city-wise as well as for the whole sample.

4.2 Some Key Findings of the Survey

Now we present a qualitative analysis of the results along with the main findings of the survey. The main findings are further validated by a quantitative analysis.

Consumption Patterns

In this section, we take a look at the overall consumption patterns of the respondents in the sample. The survey respondents spend around 48.3 per cent of their annual disposable income on consumption, which includes fruits and vegetables, apparels, accessories, jewellery and consumer durables. There is no significant variation across cities. An average of 10 per cent of the annual disposable income is spent each on house rent, recreational activities or holidays, and on education and health. Consumers save around an average 11.9 per cent of their disposable income and another 7 per cent is spent on paying various equated monthly

Figure 4.2

Percentage of Income Spent under Different Categories across Cities

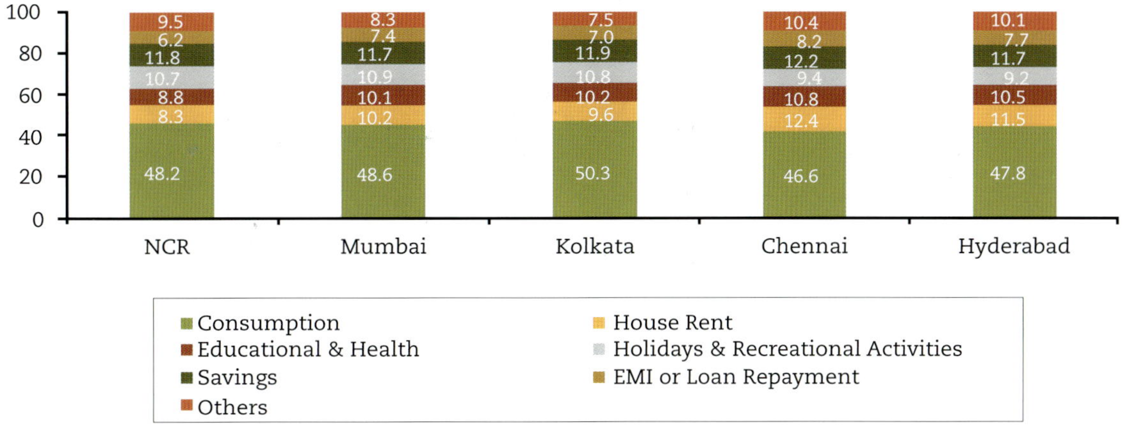

Note: "Others" primarily include utility bills, laundry bills, newspapers etc.

Source: Authors' calculations.

Figure 4.3

Percentage of Income Spent on Total Consumption and on Fruits & Vegetables across Cities

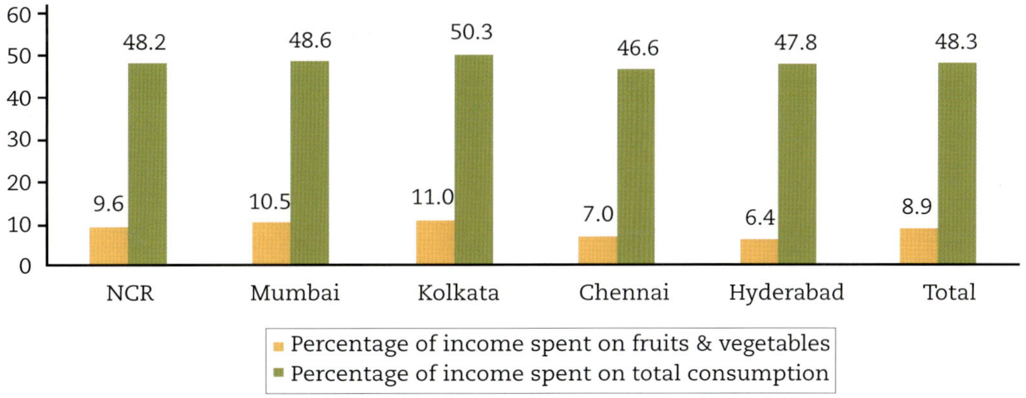

Source: Authors' calculations.

instalments. Figure 4.2 shows the percentage of income spent on different categories across cities.[2]

Since we are interested in studying the consumption patterns of fruits and vegetables primarily, we do a comparative analysis on the expenditure of households on fruits and vegetables vis-à-vis the total expenditure on consumption. While the average consumer in the sample spends around 48.3 per cent of their annual disposable income on consumption, only 8.9 per cent of their income is spent on fruits and vegetables. Figure 4.3 shows the percentage of spending on fruits and vegetables vis-à-vis the percentage of income spent on total consumption city-wise.[3]

Analysis of Intake of Fruits and Vegetables

The WHO panel on diet, nutrition and prevention of chronic diseases recommended a daily intake of at least 400 grams (or five daily servings with an average serving size of 80 grams) of fruits and vegetables, excluding potatoes, cassava and other starchy

2. Percentages in a city may not add up to 100 per cent because of missing values in each category of expenditure. The figures give a close approximation of the average expenditure on different items by a typical person.

3. The percentage of income spent on fruits and vegetables is comparatively lower in Chennai and Hyderabad as compared to other cities. However, we cannot draw any conclusion because the number of people in the upper income bracket is higher in these two cities vis-à-vis others. It is possible that the absolute amounts are close but the percentages are low in these two cities because incomes are higher.

Box 4.1

Average Daily Intake of Fruits and Vegetables

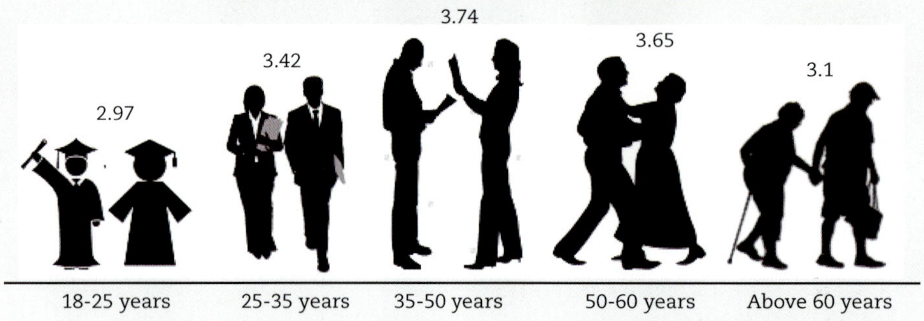

tubers to prevent diet-related chronic diseases and micronutrient deficiencies.

In this section, we present a detailed analysis of the actual intake of fruits and vegetables of the respondents in the sample. First, we present the analysis of the intake of fruits and vegetables together, followed by a detailed analysis of intake of fruits and vegetables separately.

(a) Overall Intake of Fruits and Vegetables

The average intake of vegetables is 2 servings and is higher than the average intake of fruits which is 1.5 servings on a typical day. Hence, the average intake of fruits and vegetables taken together is 3.5 servings on a typical day. Further, there are substantial variations in the intake of fruits and vegetables across different age groups, economic status, cities and diet types. There is no significant variation across gender. Since certain vegetables like onions, tomatoes, garlic and spices like ginger are an essential part of Indian dishes, this probably explains the higher average intake of vegetables compared to fruits, which are generally not a standard part of a typical diet.

> The average intake of fruits and vegetables is 3.5 servings per day which comprises 2 servings of vegetables and 1.5 servings of fruits.

As stated previously, WHO recommends 5 servings of fruits and vegetables in a typical day for an adult. If we combine the intake of fruits and vegetables, the average is 3.5 servings for the sample. The average intake of consumers in India is way below WHO recommended levels. If we do a more detailed analysis, the younger generations' intake of fruits and vegetables is even lower. The average intake is 3.3 servings for respondents in the age group 18-35 years while the average is 3.7 servings for respondents in the age group 35-60 years. Respondents in the age group 18-25 years have immensely low levels of fruits and vegetables with 2.97 servings per day (Box 4.1).

> The average intake among the students is abysmally low at 2.94 servings per day. Housewives do better in terms of fruits and vegetables intake with an average intake of 3.65 servings as compared to working persons—which is 3.5 servings per day.

Similar concerns arise when we look at the average intake of fruits and vegetables among students, which is also at an abysmally low level compared to the WHO recommendation. The average intake is 2.94 servings for a student, which is approximately 2 servings less than the recommended levels. This is a serious concern since the youth and students of this country are far from maintaining healthy standards in terms of intake of fruits and vegetables. Students, who have filled up the questionnaire, are more likely to stay away from home in hostels and it is difficult for them to store fruits and vegetables in their rooms. It would be too much to expect that students will purchase fruits and vegetables from the market. Freshly cut and packed fruits and vegetables (in salad format) are easily available in supermarkets and convenience stores such as 7-Eleven in most countries at reasonable prices but this is not the case in India. Often, students find fruits and vegetables costly and beyond their budgets. Further, hostel canteens even in private colleges do not offer the right mix of fruits and vegetables. Awareness among the student community is low and they often prefer to eat out. All these factors are a cause for concern for a country like India whose development depends on its young population.

Indian consumers across all income groups are consuming less than the 'recommended' quantity of at least 400 grams (or five daily servings with an average serving size of 80 grams) of fruits and vegetables.

Interestingly, this survey shows that housewives do better in terms of fruits and vegetables intake with an average intake of 3.65 servings as compared to the average intake of a working person, which is at 3.5 servings. It may be that housewives do get time to have fruits and vegetables in different formats since they are at home. If one compares the consumption patterns of fruits and vegetables for those who stay at home and those who are out of home, it is clear that consumption to some extent is determined by availability. In most countries, fruits and vegetables are available in different formats—frozen, chopped, tinned, juice, etc. In India, there are limited options in the processed category. Most vegetables are consumed cooked. Further, the processed category is high-priced and attracts tax. A large part of the processing is in the unorganised sector[4] and there are quality issues. A number of survey respondents felt that it is not safe to have cut fruits from roadside vendors. All these factors have led to low consumption of fruits and vegetables when a person is away from home.

Household income does play an important role in determining the average intake of fruits and vegetables. This is not surprising given the high food inflation and hence, high prices of fruits and vegetables in recent times. Table 4.2 gives the average serving of fruits and vegetables across income groups.

Table 4.2

Average Intake of Total Serving of Fruits and Vegetables across Income Groups

Income Group (in lakhs of rupees)	*Average Total Serving*
2-5	3.1
5-10	3.5
10-15	3.7
15 -25	3.9
Above 25	4

Source: Authors' calculations

4. The unorganised sector is the traditional, non-corporate sector while organised sector is the modern, corporate sector.

Income plays an important role in the consumption of fruits and vegetables—average daily intake is higher for higher income.

The average total intake of fruits and vegetables varies across cities too. Table 4.3 provides the average total serving across cities.

Table 4.3

Average Intake of Total Serving of Fruits and Vegetables across Cities

City	*Average Total Serving*
NCR	3.19
Mumbai	3.17
Kolkata	2.81
Chennai	4.35
Hyderabad	4.05

Source: Authors' calculations

There is inter-city variation in consumption of fruits and vegetables—it is the highest in Chennai and the lowest in Kolkata.

Chennai tops the list with the highest number of servings of fruits and vegetables while Kolkata is at the bottom of the cities covered in the survey. The greater number of vegetarians and the relatively higher income in the sample can partly explain the high levels of intake of fruits and vegetables in Chennai and Hyderabad.[5]

In the sample of 1,001 respondents, 526 are non-vegetarian (52.5 per cent) and 361 are vegetarian (36.1 per cent). Figure 4.4 gives the distribution of the sample by diet type across cities as well as for the overall sample. While Hyderabad has the highest number of vegetarians (109), it is closely followed by Mumbai (91) and Chennai (88). Mumbai has the

5. Though Mumbai has high number of vegetarians and Jain, but income levels are higher in Hyderabad and Chennai. Both diet types and income play a role and this is confirmed by the regression analysis in Appendix E.

Figure 4.4

Distribution of the Respondents by Diet Type across Cities (in numbers)

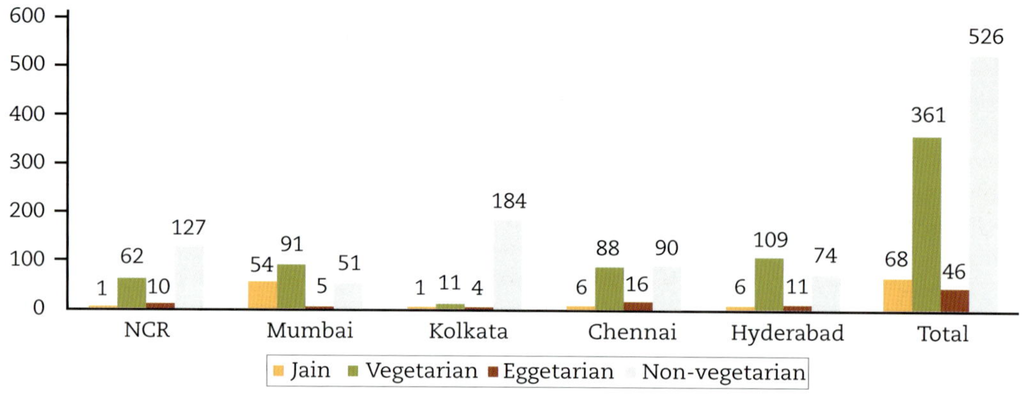

Source: Authors' calculations.

Figure 4.5

Distribution of the Respondents by the Number of Servings Consumed across Diet Types (in percentage)

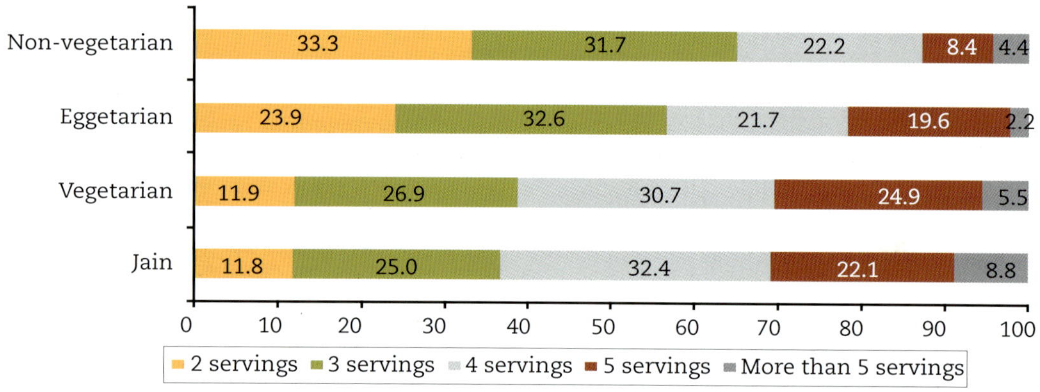

Source: Authors' calculations.

highest number of Jains (54) and Kolkata tops the list of non-vegetarians with 184 respondents.

Comparing across diet types, as is expected, vegetarians do better in terms of intake of fruits and vegetables though everyone is falling short of WHO recommended levels irrespective of the diet type. The average intake of fruits and vegetables is 3.97 servings for a person with a Jain diet, while it is 3.87 for a vegetarian, 3.43 for an eggetarian and 3.2 for a non-vegetarian. Figure 4.5 gives a detailed description of the percentage of respondents with the number of servings of fruits and vegetables across different diet types. While 33.3 per cent of the respondents who are non-vegetarian have an average of 2 servings of fruits and vegetables, only 11.9 per cent of the vegetarians have 2 servings. If one considers the WHO recommended 5 serving of fruits and vegetables, 24.9 per cent of vegetarians have 5 servings daily but the same number for non-vegetarians is abysmally low at 8.4 per cent.

> There are variations across diet types—the average daily intake of fruits and vegetables is 3.97 servings for a person with a Jain diet, while it is 3.87 servings for a vegetarian, 3.43 servings for an eggetarian and 3.2 servings for a non-vegetarian.

The findings so far hold even in the regression analysis (See Appendix E for regression results). In our regression analysis, the total number of

Figure 4.6

Distribution of the Respondents by the Number of Days they Consume Fruits in a Week across Age Groups (in percentage)

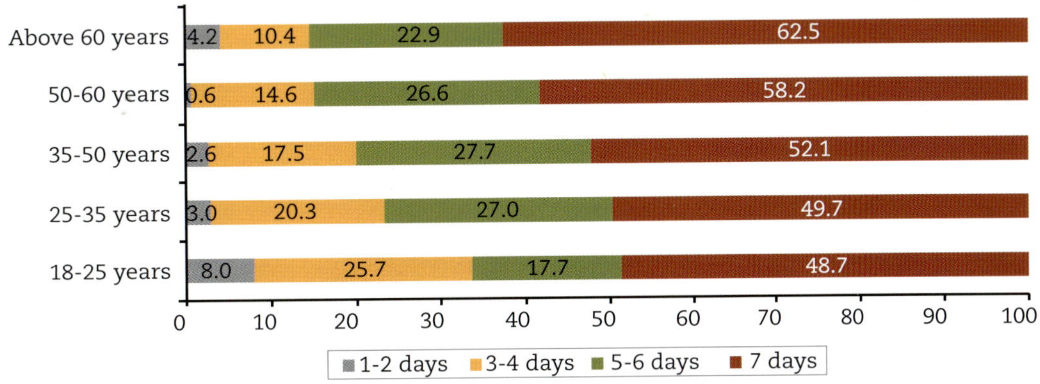

Source: Authors' calculations.

servings of fruits and vegetables is the dependent variable and the primary independent variables are annual household income, age, gender dummy,[6] diet types dummy and dummies for housewives and students (See Appendix E for a detailed list of all variables and their description). Regression Table E.1 in Appendix E shows that total servings of fruits and vegetables increases with annual household income with its coefficient being positive and significant. The coefficient for the vegetarian diet dummy is positive and significant indicating that people with a vegetarian diet consume more fruits and vegetables than consumers with a non-vegetarian diet. Moreover, the regression results indicate that the intake of fruits and vegetables is significantly lower for students than the average while the consumption of housewives is higher than the average. The coefficients for student dummy and housewife dummy are significant, with the former being negative and the latter being positive validating our descriptive analysis (see Model 3 in Regression Table E.1).

(b) Intake of Fruits

Respondents were asked to report the number of days they have fruits in a typical week. The average for the sample is 5.8 days. There are significant variations across age groups, income groups and cities. There is no significant variation across gender. The younger population consumes fruits on a lesser number of days in a typical week compared to others. While respondents in the age group 18 to 35 years eat fruits 5.6 days a week on average, respondents above the age of 35 typically have fruits on 5.9 days a week. As can be clearly seen from Figure 4.6, while 8 per cent of the respondents in the age-group 18-25 years have fruits on one or two days a week, the same number is 0.6 per cent for people in the age-group 50-60 years.[7] Similarly while 48.7 per cent of the respondents in the age-group 18-25 years have fruits on all days, the same numbers are 58.2 per cent and 62.5 per cent for the age groups 50-60 years and above 60 years respectively. Figure 4.6 shows the percentages of respondents having fruits and the number of days they are consumed in a week across different age groups. The intake of fruits and the number of days these are consumed in a week clearly increases with age.

A similar trend is observed across income groups. A person with an annual household income in the bracket INR 2-5 lakhs has fruits 5.4 days a week on an average while a person with an income greater than INR 25 lakhs has fruits 6.1 days a week. The averages for income brackets INR 5-10 lakhs, INR 10-15 lakhs and INR 15-25 lakhs are 5.8, 6.0 and 6.1 respectively. Figure 4.7 gives a detailed distribution of the percentage of respondents in each income group having fruits and on the number of days a week these are consumed. While only 39.4 per cent of the respondents in the income group INR 2-5 lakhs have fruits on all days in a week, the number is as high as 68.4 per cent for respondents with an annual income

6. A dummy variable is one that takes the value 0 or 1 to indicate the absence or presence of some categorical effect that may be expected to shift the outcome.

7. Here, percentages or proportions are considered because absolute numbers are not relevant. Nine out of 113 in the age-group 18-25 years is not the same as 9 out of 300 in the age-group 25-35 years.

Figure 4.7

Distribution of the Respondents by the Number of Days they Consume Fruits in a Week across Income Groups (in percentage)

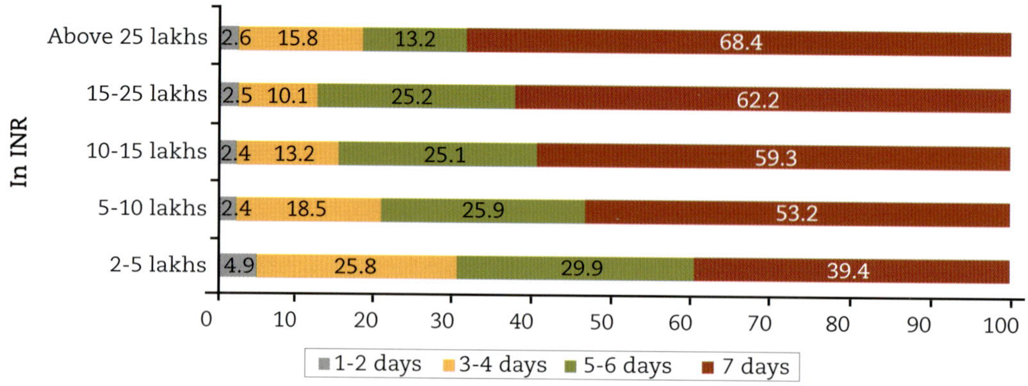

Source: Authors' calculations.

Figure 4.8

Distribution of Respondents by the Number of Servings of Fruits Per Day (in numbers)

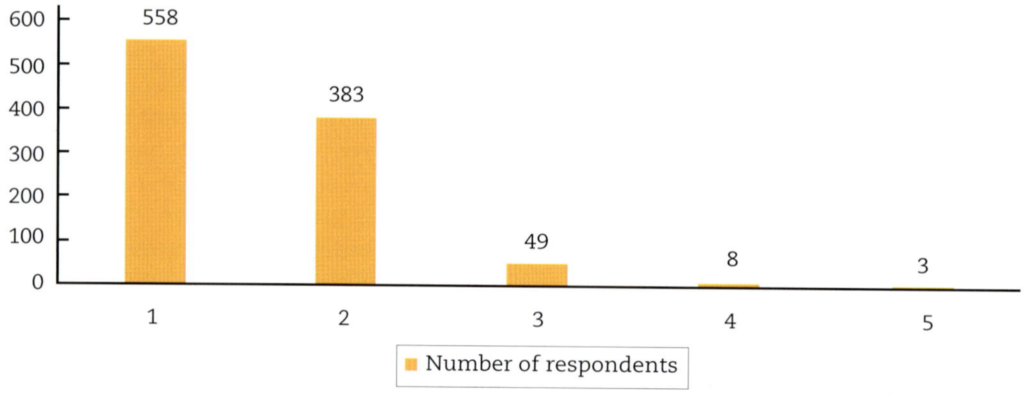

Source: Authors' calculations.

above INR 25 lakhs. This is not surprising given the high price of fruits in the Indian market.

There is also considerable variation in the number of days one has fruits in a typical week city-wise. While the average is 6.1 and 6.3 days in the NCR and Mumbai respectively, it is 5.7 and 5.8 days in Chennai and Hyderabad respectively with Kolkata being the lowest at 4.9 days. While 134 and 153 respondents have fruits on all days in the NCR and Mumbai respectively, the numbers are 62, 87 and 89 for Kolkata, Chennai and Hyderabad respectively. Figure D.5 in Appendix D provides a detailed description across cities.

However, the respondents were also asked to report the number of servings of fruits that they have on a typical day. The average intake of fruits in the sample is 1.5 servings in a day. More than half the sample has only one serving of fruit per day. Figure 4.8 shows the distribution of the number of servings of fruits in a day.

The variation in terms of servings of fruits per day across age groups and income groups is similar to the variation in terms of the number of days respondents consume fruits. Table 4.4 provides the average number of servings of fruits across age groups. It is evident that the average intake increases with age. The average for respondents above 60 years is low because of dietary restrictions.

Table 4.4

Average Intake of Serving of Fruits across Age Group

Age Group (in years)	*Average Serving of Fruits Per Day*
18-25	1.37
25-35	1.5
35- 50	1.58
50- 60	1.54
Above 60 years	1.35

Source: Authors' calculations.

Table 4.5 gives the average number of servings of fruits across income groups. As income rises, the average number of servings of fruits increases.

Table 4.5

Average Intake of Serving of Fruits across Income Groups

Income Bracket (in INR in lakhs)	*Average Serving of Fruits Per Day*
2-5	1.32
5- 10	1.52
10- 15	1.6
15- 25	1.74
Above 25	1.74

Source: Authors' calculations.

Although the average number of days in a week on which survey participants have fruits is lower in Chennai and Hyderabad as compared to the NCR and Mumbai, the average serving of fruits in a typical day is higher for Chennai and Hyderabad as opposed to NCR and Mumbai. Kolkata has the lowest per week consumption of fruits as well as the number of servings of fruits in a day. The average serving of fruits in a day is 1.82 for Chennai and 1.62 for Hyderabad, while it is 1.41 for the NCR and 1.45 for Mumbai. The average serving per day is 1.27 for Kolkata. One of the determinants that might drive this result is the dietary choice of individuals.

Across diet types, the average serving of fruits on a typical day is 1.8 for Jain, 1.6 for vegetarian, 1.4 for eggetarian and 1.4 for non-vegetarian diets. Non-vegetarians have a lesser number of servings of fruits compared to vegetarians. The average number of days in a typical week a vegetarian has fruits is 6.1 while it is 5.5 for non-vegetarians. The average for the Jain diet is 6.7 days while for eggetarian is 5.8 days.

The most consumed fruits are apples, mangoes, oranges, grapes and bananas. Lemon and lime are among the top 5 most important fruits consumed in the two southern cities, namely Hyderabad and Chennai. According to the WHO, there are five defined groups of fruits across which individuals should consume different fruits. (See Question 15.10 in the Questionnaire in Appendix C for details). Group IV, consisting of watermelons and cantaloupes, doesn't figure in the list of top five fruits consumed across cities except for Kolkata, where watermelons are among the top five fruits consumed.

The primary form in which fruits are consumed is freshly cut while a significant amount is consumed in the form of juice. In the survey, 939 respondents (93.8 per cent) said that they have freshly cut fruits, 597 (59.6 per cent) have fruits in the form of juices while 111 have canned fruits (11.1 per cent). In this question, respondents were allowed to exercise more than one option. Intake of canned fruits is significantly lower than in western countries and this is probably due to the non-availability of canned fruits in India or high prices.

(c) Intake of Vegetables

A similar trend is observed in the consumption of vegetables. The average number of days a respondent in the sample has vegetables in a week is 6.3. However, there is variation across age groups and economic condition as measured by the annual household income. As in the case of fruits, there is no variation across gender with respect to the intake of vegetables. The youth of this country is less inclined to have vegetables as compared to people belonging to older age groups. The average intake of vegetables across age groups does not fluctuate so much as compared to fruits probably because vegetables are a key part of Indian meals while fruits are optional. However, 12.4 per cent of respondents in the age group 18-25 years still have vegetables only 3 or 4 days a week while the number is only 5.7 per cent for the respondents in the age group 50-60 years as depicted in Figure 4.9. This figure shows distribution of the percentage of respondents' intake of vegetables by the number of days in a week consumed across different age groups. Clearly, the number of days one has vegetables in a week increases with age.

Given the rising prices of vegetables, income does play an important role in determining the purchase of vegetables. As depicted in Figure 4.10, while 59.2 per cent of respondents in the annual income bracket INR 2-5 lakhs have vegetables on all days, the number is 76.3 per cent for respondents in the highest income bracket. Figure 4.10 gives the distribution of respondents by the number of days in a week they have vegetables across different income groups.

There is some variation in the number of days one has vegetables in a typical week by city. While the average is 6.7 and 6.8 days in the NCR and Mumbai respectively, it is 6.1 days for Kolkata and 6 for Hyderabad with Chennai being lowest at 5.8 days.

While 165 and 179 respondents have vegetables on all days in the NCR and Mumbai respectively, the numbers are 120, 73 and 90 for Kolkata, Chennai and Hyderabad respectively. Figure D.6 in Appendix D provides a detailed description of the number of days per week of vegetables intake across cities.

The respondents were also asked to report the number of servings of vegetables that they have on a typical day. The average intake of vegetables in the sample is 2 servings in a day. Figure 4.11 shows the distribution of the number of servings of vegetables in a day across the sample.

Figure 4.9

Distribution of the Respondents by the Number of Days they Consume Vegetables in a Week Across Age Groups (in percentage)

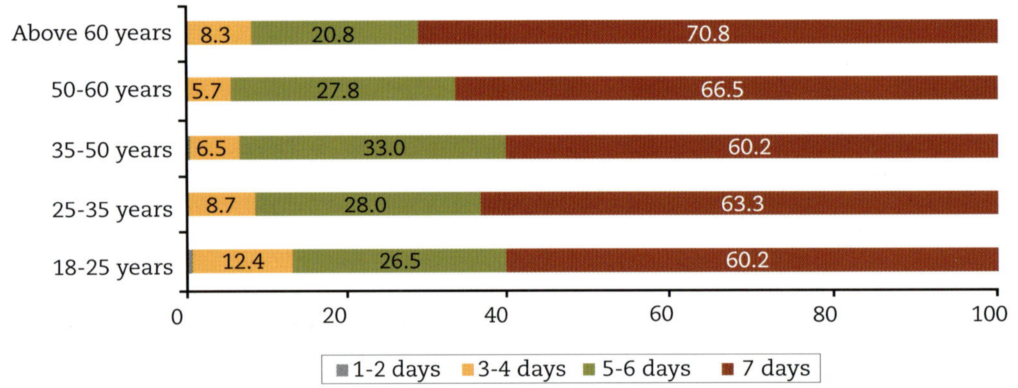

Source: Authors' calculations.

Figure 4.10

Distribution of the Respondents by the Number of Days they Consume Vegetables in a Week Across Income Groups (in percentage)

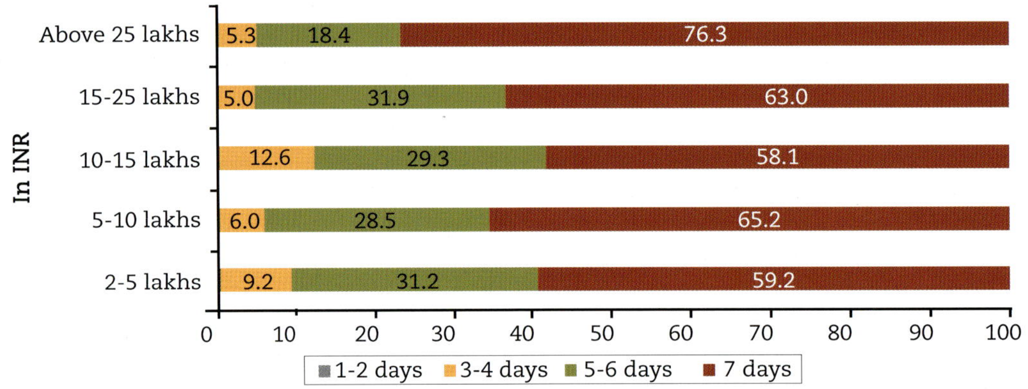

Source: Authors' calculations.

Figure 4.11

Dictribution of Respondents by the Number of Servings of Vegetables they Intake in a Day (in numbers)

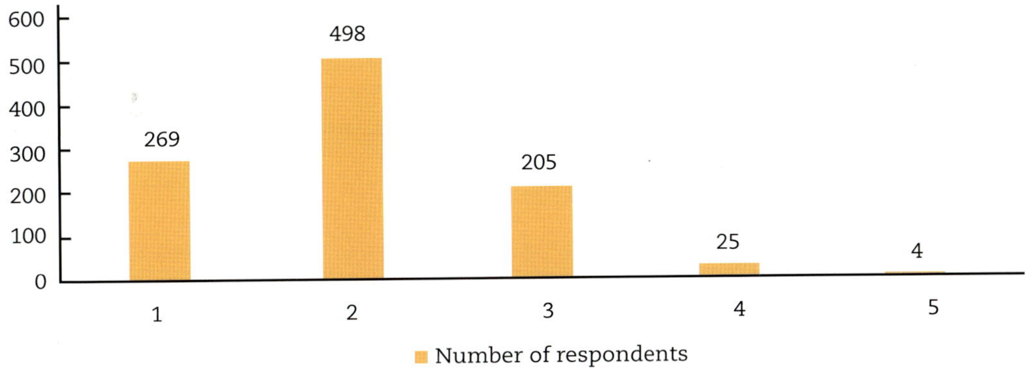

Source: Authors' calculations.

Table 4.6 provides the average number of servings of vegetables across age groups. As evident from the table, the average across age groups is inverted U-shaped with respondents in the age group 35-50 having the highest number of servings in a day, the primary reason being that due to dietary restrictions, the average intake starts declining once a certain age is reached.

Table 4.6

Average Intake of Serving of Vegetables across Age Group

Age Group (in years)	*Average Serving of Vegetables Per Day*
18-25	1.6
25-35	1.92
35-50	2.16
50-60	2.12
Above 60	1.75

Source: Authors' calculations.

Table 4.7 gives the average number of servings of vegetables across income groups. As income rises, there is a clear increasing trend in the intake of vegetables, confirming the fact that there is a positive correlation between income and the intake of vegetables.

If we consider the average number of servings of vegetables in a day across cities, Chennai tops the list with 2.5 servings followed by Hyderabad (2.4), NCR (1.78), Mumbai (1.72) and Kolkata with 1.54 servings.

Among the most consumed vegetables in the country are cucumbers, cauliflower, onions, tomatoes and garlic. Green chilli is among the most consumed vegetable in Hyderabad and Chennai whereas it is not among the top 5 vegetables consumed in other cities. WHO not only recommends the serving size of fruits and vegetables an adult should take, it also recommends having vegetables across all categories. There are four categories of vegetables (See Question 15.9 in the questionnaire in Appendix C for details). Consumption of Group III vegetables (as described by WHO), which contains spinach and other leafy vegetables, is low in India.

Table 4.7

Average Intake of Serving of Vegetables across Income Groups

Income Bracket (in INR lakhs)	*Average Serving of Vegetables Per Day*
2-5	1.77
5- 10	2.02
10- 15	2.07
15- 25	2.21
Above 25	2.26

Source: Authors' calculations.

Across diet types, the average number of servings of vegetables on a typical day is 2.18 for Jain, 2.27 for vegetarian, 2 for eggetarian and 1.8 for non-vegetarian. The non-vegetarians, as expected, have a lesser number of servings of vegetables as compared to vegetarians. The average number of days in a typical week a vegetarian has vegetables is 6.7 while it is 6.0 for non-vegetarians. The average for Jain diet is 6.9 days and for eggetarian diet, it is 6.3 days.

The primary form in which Indian consumers prefer to have vegetables is cooked. While 976 (97.5 per cent) respondents have vegetables in cooked form, 723

Figure 4.12

Distribution of Respondents as per the Source of Awareness about Health Benefits of having Fruits and Vegetables (in numbers)

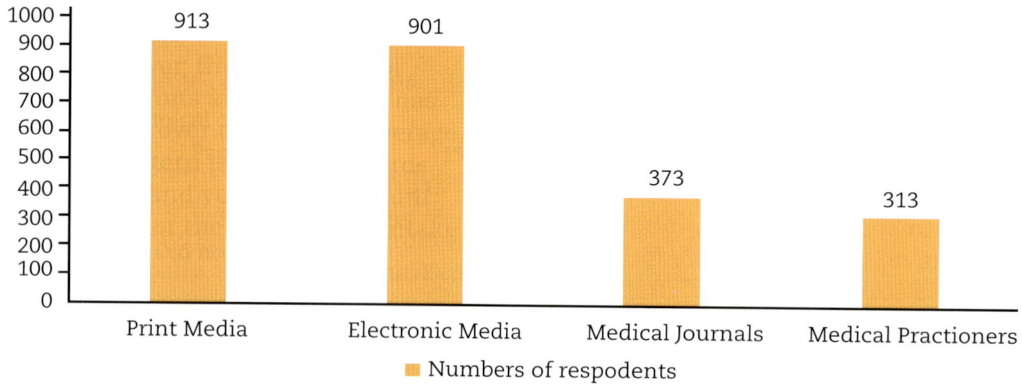

Source: Authors' calculations.

(72.2 per cent) have vegetables chopped raw and 157 (15.7 per cent) respondents have them in juice form. Respondents were allowed to choose from multiple options.

> The level of awareness about the WHO recommended daily intake of at least 400 grams (or five daily servings with an average serving size of 80 grams) of fruits and vegetables is low—89 per cent of the respondents are not aware.

Awareness of Indian Consumers of WHO Recommendation

The survey asked the respondents whether they are aware of the WHO recommendation of having 5 servings of fruits and vegetables in a day. Eighty-nine per cent are not aware of any such recommendation. Among those who are aware, more than 50 per cent of them have educational qualifications of postgraduate and above. On the contrary when asked whether they are aware of the benefits of having fruits and vegetables, a massive 95 per cent of the respondents are aware of the benefits. The top 3 benefits as suggested by the consumers are: (a) good for health (nourishment, eyesight, skin, etc.), (b) adds roughage to diet, source of fibres, proteins, calcium and other components, (c) good for blood circulation and purification and the digestive system. Figure 4.12 provides the primary sources of information about the benefits of having fruits and vegetables and their corresponding frequencies. Media (both print and electronic) plays an important role in terms of creating awareness among consumers about the advantages of having fruits and vegetables.

> Around 50 per cent of those aware of the WHO recommendations have educational qualification of post graduate and above.

> Almost 95 per cent of the respondents are aware of the benefits of fruits and vegetables.

> Print and electronic media are key sources of information.

Reasons for Not Being Able to Meet the WHO Standards

A natural question that arises at this juncture is if consumers are aware of the benefits of having fruits and vegetables, why is the consumption way short of the recommended levels? The results surprisingly point out that lifestyle is the most important factor that acts as a hindrance in meeting the standards. A busy work life, coupled with long working hours, is the major constraint for not meeting the WHO recommendation. This is followed by seasonal availability of fruits and vegetables and the cost of

Figure 4.13

Distribution of Respondents as per the Reasons Given for Not Being Able to Meet WHO Recommendation (in numbers)

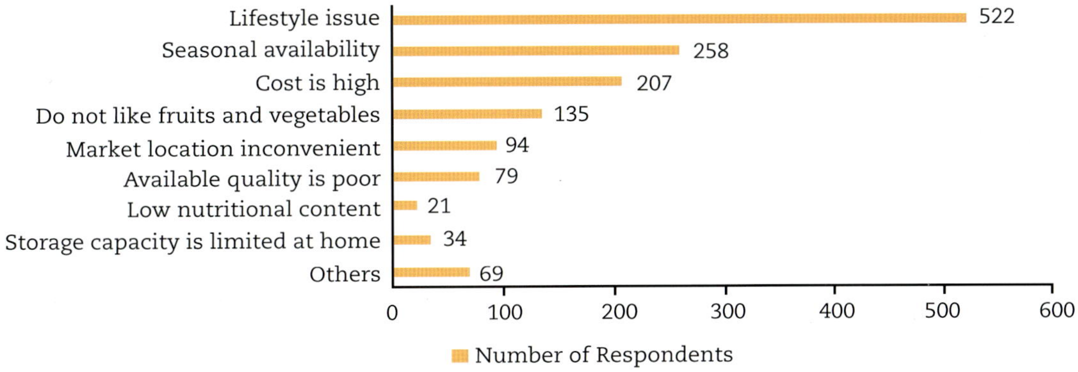

Note: "Others" primarily include strict preference for non-vegetarian food or junk food.

Source: Authors' calculations.

buying them. Figure 4.13 presents the reasons for not meeting the WHO recommended intake of fruits and vegetables and the corresponding frequency of response.[8]

Lifestyle is the topmost reason for low consumption of fruits and vegetables across all age groups but more so among the younger cohort (18-35 years) and respondents in the NCR.

The next two important reasons for low consumption of fruits and vegetables are seasonal availability and high cost.

Table 4.8

Distribution of Respondents Reporting Lifestyle as an Issue for Not Meeting WHO Standards across Cities (in numbers)

City	Number of Respondents
NCR	156
Mumbai	87
Kolkata	130
Chennai	79
Hyderabad	70

Source: Authors' calculations.

A more detailed analysis shows that although lifestyle is an important issue for not meeting the WHO standards and is prevalent across all age groups, it is more acute among the younger generation. While 56.7 per cent of the respondents in the age group between 18-35 years think lifestyle is the issue, only 48.7 per cent of the respondents in the age group above 35 years feel so. Further, there are variations across cities (see Table 4.8).

Criteria for Purchase of Fruits and Vegetables

A very important thing to understand is the criteria on which consumers base their decision to buy fruits and vegetables. Quality and freshness of the product are the top most criteria and is way ahead of others. The second most important criterion is price. Figure 4.14 shows the frequency of responses across different criteria for the overall sample. Given quality and freshness is the most important criterion for Indian consumers, they still feel that local market or push carts have fresher fruits and vegetables as compared to organised retail stores.

Purchase of Fruits and Vegetables

Food and grocery retailing in India is highly unorganised and fragmented. As a result, Indian consumers have relied mostly on push carts or

8. Respondents were allowed to tick all appropriate reasons.

Figure 4.14

Distribution of Sample According to Criteria for Purchase of Fruits and Vegetables (in numbers)

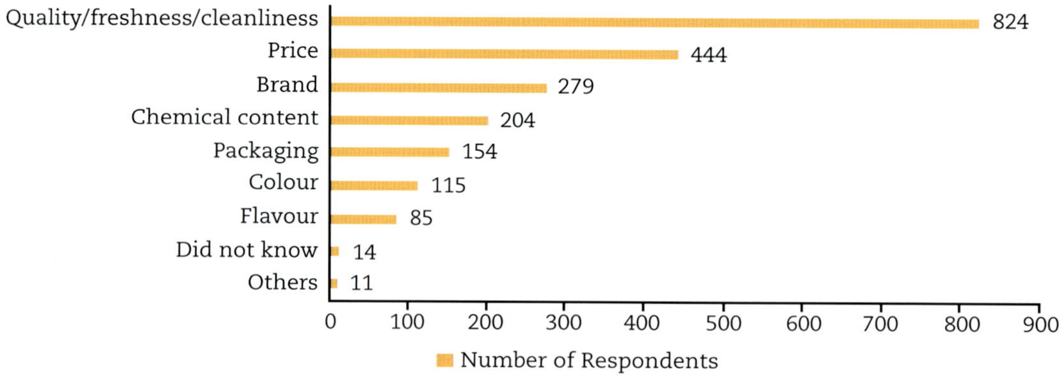

Note: "Others" primarily include nutrition content, seasonal availability.

Source: Authors' calculations.

> Quality and freshness of the product are the most important criteria based on which consumers purchase fruits and vegetables.

local markets to purchase fruits and vegetables. The entry of organised retail in the fruits and vegetables segments is recent. However, Indian consumers still prefer buying fruits and vegetables from the local market or push carts or both, despite the presence of organised retail stores in the selected metro cities (See Table 4.9).

Table 4.9

Distribution of Respondents According to Shopping Place for Fruits and Vegetables (in numbers)

Shopping Place	*Number of Respondents*
Push cart	189
Push cart & local market	2
Push cart & wholesale market	1
Local market	534
Local market & organised retailer	2
Local market & wholesale market	1
Organised market (e.g. Big Bazaar)	147
Organised market & wholesale market	1
Wholesale market	96
Don't know	28
Total	1,001

Source: Authors' calculations.

The pattern of consumption of fruits and vegetables may differ if they are purchased by a house help vis-à-vis by the respondent or his/her family member. One may presume that house helps may not be too aware of the benefits of consumption of fruits and vegetables and may not purchase them and hence, the consumption might be lower. The survey showed that this is not the case. Consumption of fruits and vegetables do not differ significantly if bought by a house help rather than by a family member. For 141 respondents (14.1 per cent) in the sample, house helps purchase fruits and vegetables while the rest either purchase them on their own or other family members make the purchase. Figure 4.15 shows that house helps buy fruits and vegetables primarily in the two southern cities and this may be due to the large number of respondents in the high-income brackets in the two cities in the sample as opposed to others.

> Indian consumers prefer to buy fruits and vegetables from the local markets (53.3 per cent) and push carts (18.8 per cent).

This result is also validated by the regression analysis in Appendix E. In regression Table E.1, house help dummy takes a value of 1 if house helps make purchases. The coefficient is insignificant validating our claim (See Model 4 in Regression Table E.1 in Appendix E).

Awareness about Adulterants in Fruits and Vegetables

Indian consumers are well aware of the presence of different adulterants in fruits and vegetables.

Figure 4.15

Distribution of Respondents as per the Purchase Incidence of Fruits and Vegetables across Cities (in numbers)

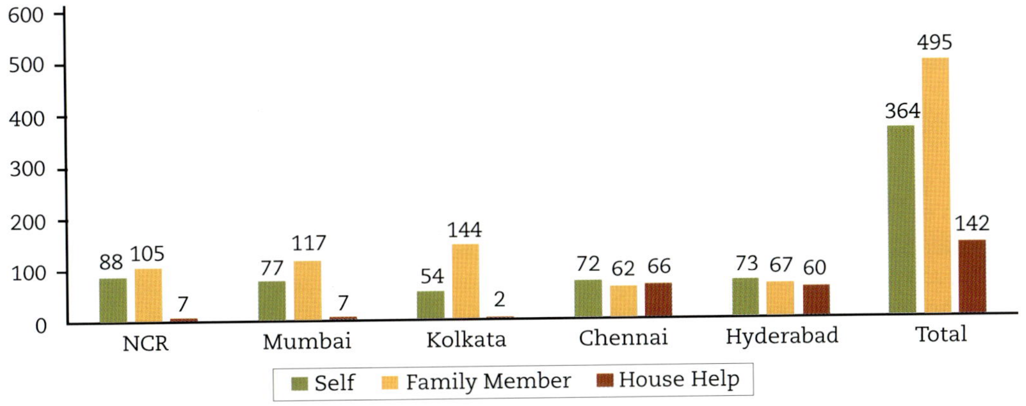

Source: Authors' calculations.

Figure 4.16

Distribution of Respondents as per their Awareness of Presence of Adulterants in Fruits and Vegetables (in numbers)

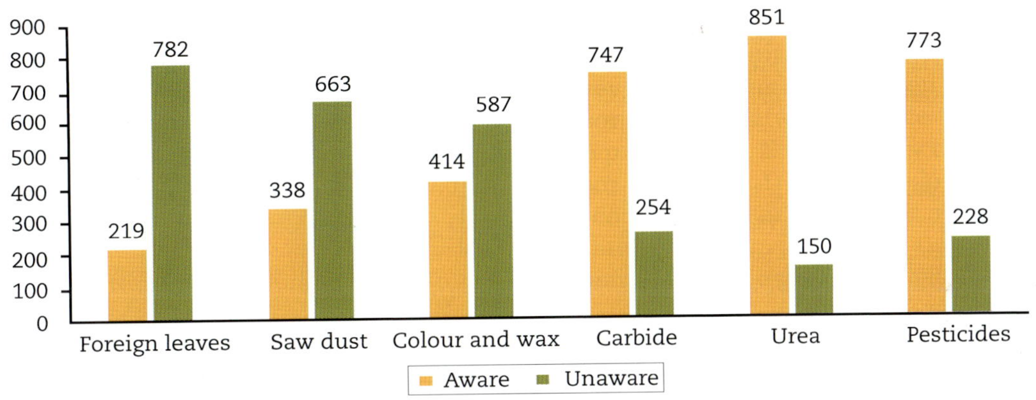

Source: Authors' calculations.

Nine hundred and seventy four (974) out of 1,001 respondents (97.3 per cent) are aware of the presence of adulterants in fruits and vegetables produced in India. 851 respondents are aware of the presence of urea in fruits and vegetables (85 per cent) while 773 are aware of the presence of pesticides in fruits and vegetables (77.2 per cent). Figure 4.16 shows the frequency of awareness in the sample about the presence of different adulterants in fruits and vegetables.

97.3 per cent consumers are aware of the presence of adulterants in fruits and vegetables.

The number of respondents claiming they are affected by the presence of adulterants in fruits and vegetables are 984 (98.3 per cent). To tackle this problem, the main method used is to clean it very well before consuming. While 534 respondents clean it and consume (53.3 per cent), 386 buy these from only select outlets (38.5 per cent), which they believe stock fruits and vegetables with less adulterant content while 291 (29.1 per cent) buy only organic products. Figure 4.17 shows the frequency of different ways respondents tackle the problem of adulterants.

Figure 4.17

Distribution of Respondents as per their Approach to Tackle the Problem of Adulterants in Fruits and Vegetables (in numbers)

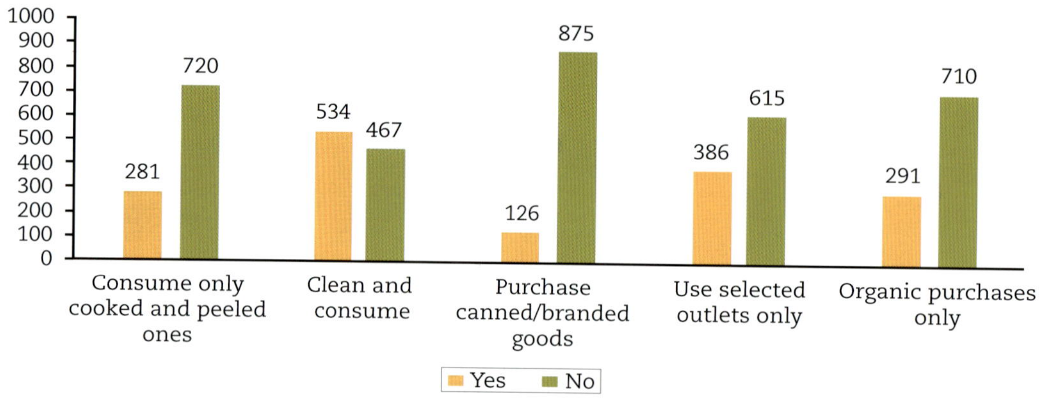

Source: Authors' calculations.

To tackle the problem of adulterants in fruits and vegetables, 53.3 per cent of the respondents clean them thoroughly before consumption; 38.5 per cent buy them from selected outlets while 29.1 per cent buy organic products.

A majority of Indian consumers (75.6 per cent) are willing to purchase organic products as they consider them to be of better quality and free of pesticides and chemicals. However, only 29.1 per cent of the respondents actually buy organic products.

Preference for Buying Organic versus Inorganic and Branded versus Unbranded Fruits and Vegetables

Today, Indian consumers are more willing to purchase organic products instead of inorganic ones. This is because consumers are quite aware of the presence of pesticides and other adulterants in fruits and vegetables as shown previously. 757 respondents are willing to buy organic fruits and vegetables (75.6 per cent) and primary reasons they cited are that organic products are of better quality, chemical and pesticides free and hygienic. Those who prefer to buy inorganic products prefer to do so because, according to them, organic products are expensive and not easily available. Figure 4.18 shows the distribution of preferences for purchasing organic fruits and vegetables across cities. The preference for organic products increases with income. While 70 per cent of the respondents in the income group INR 2-5 lakhs prefer organic products, it is 74 per cent, 81 per cent, 81 per cent and 89 per cent for income groups INR 5-INR 10 lakhs, INR 10-15 lakhs, INR 15-25 lakhs and above INR 25 lakhs respectively.

The gap between the willingness to buy and actual purchase is due to non-availability of organic fruits and vegetables.

An important point to be noted is that although 757 respondents (75.6 per cent) are willing to buy organic fruits and vegetables (see Figure 4.18), only 291 (29.1 per cent) actually buy organic fruits and vegetables (see Figure 4.17). Respondents reported that they are even willing to pay a higher price for buying organic fruits and vegetables. Around 58 per cent of the respondents who prefer to buy organic products are willing to pay a higher price for these.[9] This suggests that there is a gap between preferences and actual purchase and this is most likely to be because of the non-availability of organic fruits and vegetables.

9. Consumers reported that they are willing to pay more for organic fruits and vegetables but did not know how much more. A possibility is that the additional amount that they are willing to pay is still short of the price of organic fruits and vegetables.

Figure 4.18

Distribution of Respondents According to their Preference for Buying Organic *versus* Inorganic Fruits and Vegetables (in numbers)

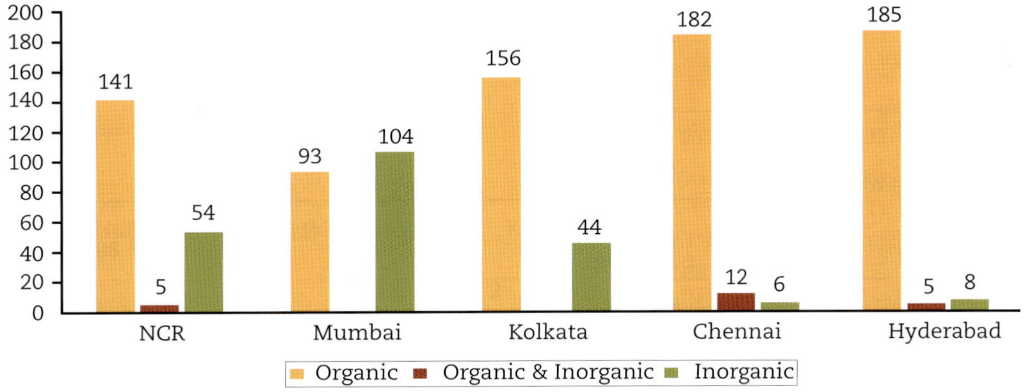

Source: Authors' calculations.

Figure 4.19

Distribution of Respondents According to their Preference for Buying Branded and Unbranded Fruits and Vegetables (in numbers)

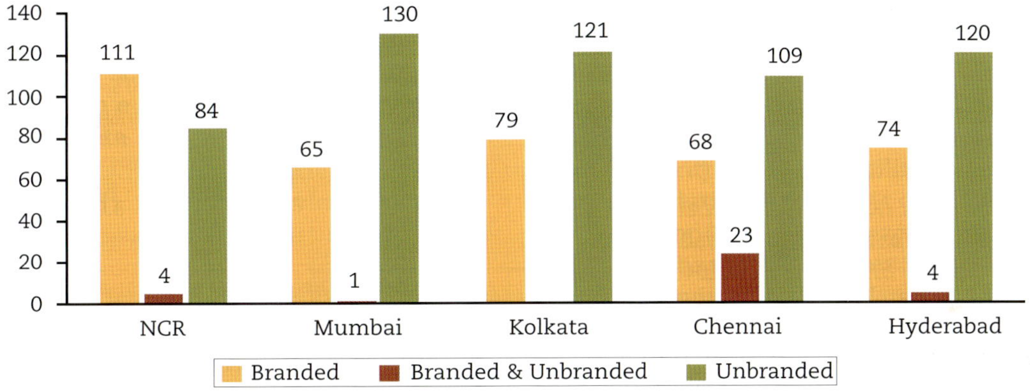

Source: Authors' calculations.

Hence, a potential market for organic fruits and vegetables remains untapped.

Although Indian consumers are willing to buy organic fruits and vegetables, they prefer to buy unbranded rather than branded fruits and vegetables. 564 respondents (56.3 per cent) indicated a willingness to purchase unbranded products while 397 indicated a preference for branded products (39.7 per cent). Figure 4.19 shows the distribution of preferences for purchasing branded and unbranded fruits and vegetables across the sample as well as across cities. Respondents feel that branded products are overpriced, contain preservatives and are not always fresh and chemical free while those preferring branded products feel that they are of good quality and hence, good for health. People in the upper income brackets typically prefer to purchase branded products. While 29 per cent of the respondents in the income bracket of INR 2-5 lakhs annually would prefer to buy branded products, 53 per cent of the respondents with an annual income above INR 15 lakhs prefer branded products.

> A majority of the respondents are willing to purchase non-branded fruits and vegetables as they feel that branded products are over-priced, contain preservatives and are not always fresh and chemical free.

Nutritional Supplements

Since survey participants fall short of consuming the WHO recommended quantity of fruits and vegetables,

Figure 4.20

Distribution of Respondents Using Nutritional Supplements across Cities (in numbers)

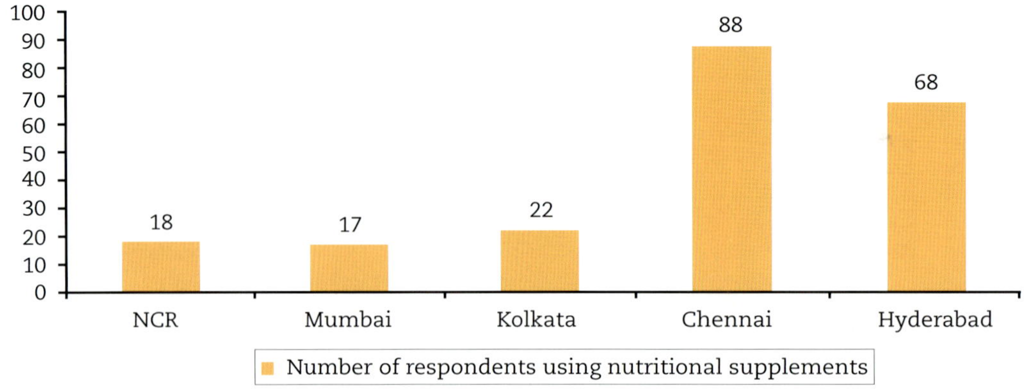

Source: Authors' calculations.

it is important to understand whether they are complementing the shortfall in consumption through dietary supplements. If they do so, then the shortfall in actual consumption may not lead to adverse health impacts.

> The use of nutritional supplements is quite low in India and the consumption of supplements varies across cities. It is relatively high in southern cities (Chennai and Hyderabad) and is the lowest in Mumbai.

> The intake of health supplements is the lowest among the younger cohort, especially students. It is the highest among vegetarians.

The survey showed that the usage of nutritional supplements is quite low in India. Only 213 out of 1,001 respondents (21.3 per cent) consume nutritional supplements. Figure 4.20 gives the distribution of nutritional supplements city-wise. The usage is relatively higher in the southern cities as compared to other cities. The usage of nutritional supplements does not vary dramatically across gender and income groups.

Although the actual intake of supplements is low, consumers are aware of the presence of such supplements in the market. For example, 756 respondents (75.5 per cent) are aware of the Amway Nutrilite health supplement range and the awareness is almost uniform across cities.

The younger generation does as poorly in the intake of health supplements as in the intake of fruits and vegetables. Only 12.4 per cent of the respondents in the age group 18-25 years have health supplements, while 22.4 per cent of the respondents in the age group above 25 have nutritional supplements. Students fare even worse. Only 8.8 per cent of students have nutritional supplements while 18.7 per cent of working consumers and 32.7 per cent of housewives have nutritional supplements. This is a major concern since students have abysmally low levels of fruits and vegetables as well as health supplements.

If we look across diet types, usage of nutritional supplements is higher among vegetarians as compared to non-vegetarians. The proportion of vegetarians having nutritional supplements is 27.4 per cent while 17.3 per cent of non-vegetarians have supplements. The trend is similar to the trend in the intake of fruits and vegetables among the vegetarians and non-vegetarians.

Respondents prefer to buy health supplements from general stores or from a pharmacy. Figure 4.21 shows the preferred source of purchase of health supplements across different outlets.

Figure 4.21

Distribution of the Respondents as per the Source of Purchase of Nutritional Supplements (in numbers)

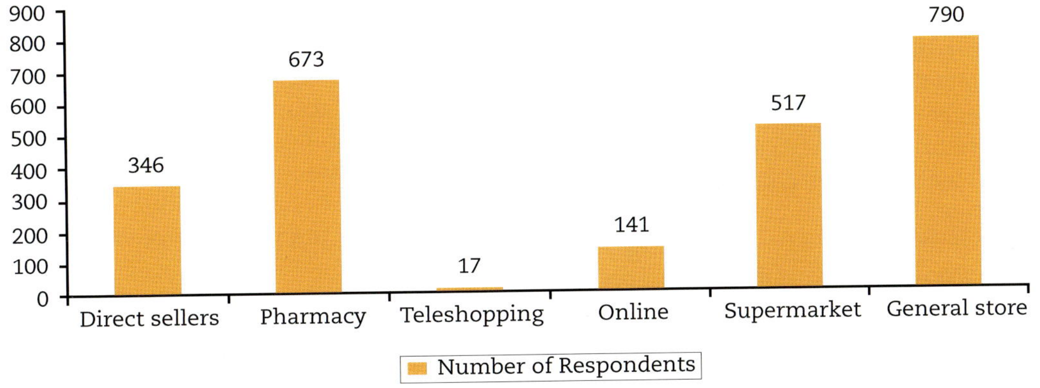

Source: Authors' calculations.

> Respondents prefer to buy health supplements from general stores and pharmacies.

Health Condition of Respondents

Dietary restrictions due to a certain health issue or allergies can prevent consumers from consuming fruits and vegetables. However, in our sample, only 11 per cent of the respondents have food allergies or dietary restrictions. Hence, dietary restrictions cannot explain the low intake of fruits and vegetables. This claim is validated by the regression results in Appendix E. The dummy for dietary restriction is insignificant, validating our claim (See Model 4 in Regression Table E.1 in Appendix E). A detailed analysis of the health condition of the respondents is provided in Appendix F.

Awareness of Policy and Regulatory Standards

Indian consumers are not too aware of their rights under the Consumer Protection Act, 1986, or of food safety regulations as per the FSSA, 2006. While only 302 respondents (30.2 per cent) are aware of consumer protection rights under the Consumer Protection Act, 1986, 336 consumers (33.5 per cent) are aware of food safety regulations as per the FSSA, 2006. Figure 4.22 shows the level of awareness city-wise.

Figure 4.22

Number of Respondents Aware of the Consumer Protection Rights and Food Safety Regulations across Different Cities

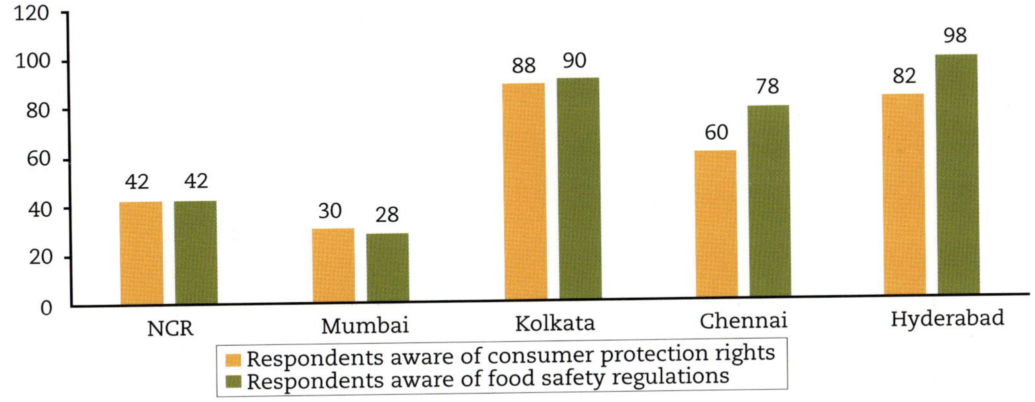

Source: Authors' calculations.

4.3 The Key Takeaways of the Survey

This survey clearly points out that the average intake of fruits and vegetables in India falls way below WHO recommended levels. Although vegetarians do better in terms of the intake of fruits and vegetables compared to non-vegetarians, a majority of the population still falls short of the recommended levels. The intake among youth and students is at an alarmingly low level, which is a matter of serious concern since the health of youth is crucial for the future growth and development of a developing country like India, whose growth is dependent on the strength of its young population. There is an immediate need to increase awareness among youth and students about the benefits of eating more fruits and vegetables. Income plays an important role in determining the intake of fruits and vegetables and this is not surprising, given high food inflation and the high prices of fruits and vegetables. There is an urgent need for the government to frame policies to control the prices of fruits and vegetables so that consumers are able to maintain a healthy diet and consume more fruits and vegetables. Although consumers are aware of the benefits of having fruits and vegetables, there is still a need to increase awareness of WHO recommended servings. Moreover, there is a strong preference among consumers for organic products because of their awareness of the presence of various adulterants in fruits and vegetables produced in India. However, there seems to be a constraint in the availability of organic produce in India. The survey also shows that consumption of nutritional supplements is low in India.

The next section focuses on the barriers in the food supply chain and its impact on consumption.

5

Barriers in the Supply Chain and their Impact on Consumption

The discussions in the previous sections highlight the fact that India is one of the largest producers of fruits and vegetables. However, over the years, productivity has not increased and the extent of processing and value addition is low.[1] According to the Ministry of Food Processing Industries, the commercial processing of fruits and vegetables stands at 2.02 per cent of the total production in India.[2] This is also evident from the survey conducted, which shows that consumers have limited choices in terms of frozen products, processed products and cut fruits and vegetables. Around 76 per cent of the respondents mentioned that they are willing to buy organic fruits and vegetables, but actual purchases were only 29 per cent because of the lack of availability of such products. Thus, there is a demand-supply gap. A country with a large production base is unable to meet consumer requirements. This has led to consumption of fruits and vegetables below the WHO recommended daily intake.

The level of food processing in India is low and the supply chain is fragmented. About 18 per cent of fruits and vegetables get wasted in the supply chain and there is a lack of cold chain infrastructure.

It is well-known that the supply chain in India is highly fragmented, marked by the presence of multiple intermediaries and about 18 per cent of the fruits and vegetables get wasted in the supply chain.[3] There are other issues such as the seasonality of production and crop failures, which are problems faced by almost all countries. However, in developed countries, seasonality is cushioned by better supply chain management, storage facilities and imports. In the case of India, seasonality leads to sudden shortages and rise in prices. This adversely affects consumers. For instance, onion, which is a vegetable used commonly in the Indian diet, saw an almost 85 per cent increase in the year-on-year prices in October 2015,[4] due to the drought that led to the failure of the *kharif* crop.[5] The prices of a number of fruits and vegetables such as onions, peas and tomatoes have risen steadily despite a reduction in the general inflation rate. Hoarding and unscrupulous trade practices lead to a rise in prices of essential vegetables such as onions.

A number of studies have shown that the lack of cold chain infrastructure leads to wastage. The National Centre for Cold Chain Development (NCCD) and National Bank for Agriculture and Rural Development (NABARD) Consultancy Service (2015) data show that while India has adequate cold storage capacities, there is a huge demand-supply gap. The establishment of cold chain infrastructure has been non-uniform across the states, with Uttar Pradesh, West Bengal and Gujarat having substantial storage capacities, while the north-eastern states of Sikkim, Manipur and Mizoram have very low storage capacities. There are hardly any storage facilities at the *mandis* and there is significant shortage of pack houses and refrigerated vehicles. India has only 249 pack houses and most of them are used for exports. Thus, there are gaps in the cold chain infrastructure which lead to wastage.

Many fruits and vegetables such as apples, peaches, tomatoes, cucumber, etc. have identified with multiple pesticides in the past.

During the survey, consumers raised concerns about the quality of produce, the presence of pesticides and other adulterants in fruits and vegetables. Apples, peaches, strawberries, spinach, cucumber, and potatoes are some of the fruits and vegetables that have been identified with multiple pesticides in the past.[6] A report by the Ministry of Agriculture showed that there had been an almost two-fold increase in the number of samples having pesticides

1. In the Indian context, processing of food products refers to transformation of raw food items through physical/ chemical and other industrial processes.
2. Press Release, Ministry of Food Processing Industries (May 2015). Available at: *http://www.mofpi.nic.in/H_Dwld.aspx?KYEwmOL+HGqTV0f1VSVZLW3VlDC+YHsvTxu0wQ5UZV6A2b8EA0NTsw==* (accessed on 30 November 2015).
3. Yes Bank Limited and Ministry of Food Processing Industries (2014) and Mukherjee et al. (2014).
4. Calculated using data from Office of Economic Advisor, Department of Industrial Policy and Promotion, Government of India. Available at: *http://www.eaindustry.nic.in/home.asp* (accessed on 8 December 2015).
5. *http://www.dnaindia.com/india/report-maharashtra-unseasonal-rains-hit-rabbi-crop-nashik-farmers-worried-2148244* (accessed on 30 November 2015).
6. *http://food.ndtv.com/food-drinks/the-12-most-pesticide-contaminated-fruits-and-vegetables-of-2015-752555* (accessed on 9 December 2015).

above the permitted maximum residue level (MRL) in vegetables, fruits, meat and spices in the past seven years. In 2008-09, 1.4 per cent of samples tested failed the MRL test (183 out of 13,348 samples); the figure went up to 2.6 per cent in 2014-15 (543 out of 20,618 samples). The samples were picked up from *mandis*, retail shops and farm gates. In fact, the samples picked up from *mandis* showed much higher levels of MRL than samples from farm gates.[7] The Centre for Disease Control and Prevention under the US Department of Health and Human Services conducted a study in January 2015 as part of its Morbidity and Mortality Weekly Report and found that a mysterious and sometimes fatal brain disease that has afflicted children in Bihar, India, since 1995 could be linked to a toxic substance in litchi fruits.[8]

Data on the website of the US Food and Drug Administration shows that it rejected more imports from India than from any other country in the first five months of 2015. In fact, many agriculture products from India were rejected in the US since January 2015. These include vegetables such as capsicum, which contained salmonella, and coriander, and fruits such as oranges.[9]

The survey participants pointed out that our produce, which is rejected in other countries, is being sold in the domestic market. They cited the example of the Alphanso mango, which was sold in the domestic market at a lower price after the consignment was rejected by countries in the European Union (EU) because of the presence of pesticides and insecticides in 2014.[10] One of the key problems related to this is supply chain traceability. In India, the products cannot be traced back to the farmer and the FSSA, 2006 is not applicable to farmers. Further, food safety and standards are not uniformly implemented across the different states.

The fragmentation in the supply chain is the result of several regulations affecting direct sourcing, inter-state mobility of agriculture produce, etc. First, some of the states have not adopted the model APMC Act and, therefore, they do not allow direct sourcing and contract farming. This has led to fragmentation in the supply chain. Second, there are inter-state barriers on the movement of fruits and vegetables. Waiting at inter-state check posts causes delays in movement. Since most fruits and vegetables are perishable, it leads to wastage. Third, in India, high tariffs are imposed on import of fruits and vegetables. In the year 2015, vegetables like onions, cauliflower, broccoli, carrots and green chillies attract an import tariff as high as 30 per cent while garlic attracts a tariff of 100 per cent.[11] Oranges and lemons attract a tariff of 40 per cent, and other fruits like bananas, pineapples, watermelons and papayas attract a tariff of 30 per cent.[12] In case of drought, crop failures and other calamities, it takes the government a lot of time to allow imports, which leads to a price rise. Further, custom clearance processes are slow due to multiple clearance authorities and lack of mechanisation, and often, the stock left at the port is wasted due to delays.[13]

Fourth, organised retailers and manufacturers globally not only help to set up the supply chain for fruits and vegetables, they also train farmers in best farm practices.[14] However, in India, the food and grocery sector is largely non-corporate. There are FDI restrictions on multi-brand food and grocery retail. Moreover, some states do not allow direct sourcing. Due to the complex policy, global food and grocery retailers have shown little interest in investing in India. If global companies are not allowed to set up the entire supply chain and run their best business model, they are unlikely to invest in the fruit and vegetable supply chain in India. Unless global retailers invest in India, international small and medium manufacturers will not invest in the fruit and vegetable processing sector of India, thus limiting the choices for consumers.

Fifth, the high tax on processed fruits and vegetables and the variations across states discourage processing. It also raises the price for consumers.

---

7. *http://www.agricoop.nic.in/imagedefault/Annl_rpt_2015.pdf* (accessed on 9 December 2015).
8. *http://www.cdc.gov/mmwr/pdf/wk/mm6403.pdf* (accessed on 9 December 2015).
9. *http://www.accessdata.fda.gov/scripts/importrefusals/* (accessed on 9 December 2015).
10. *http://wtocentre.iift.ac.in/ebulletin/India's%20Trade%20News%20and%20Views%2024%20April%20to%208%20May%202014.pdf* (accessed on 9 December 2015).
11. *http://www.cbec.gov.in/resources//htdocs-cbec/customs/cs-tariff2015-16/chap-7.pdf* (accessed on 3 December 2015).
12. *http://www.cbec.gov.in/resources//htdocs-cbec/customs/cs-tariff2015-16/chap-8.pdf* (accessed on 3 December 2015).
13. *http://www.livemint.com/Multimedia/NnxmmzazpjHLnZ8WeIg0ZN/Food-stocks-go-waste-while-India-fusses-about-food-security.html* (assessed on 3 December 2015).
14. The case of Brazil - *http://www.economistinsights.com/sites/default/files/Accenture_Agribusiness_ENGLISH.pdf* (accessed on 9 December 2015).

Sixth, the regulatory regime for food products in India is still evolving despite the enactment of the FSSA, 2006, and the establishment of the FSSAI. For instance, the FSSAI's advisories on product approval for non-standardised food products were arbitrary and changed frequently. As a result the Supreme Court in its order dated 19 August 2015, had declared these advisories as "being arbitrary and hence illegal".[15] Consequently, the FSSAI had to stop the product approval process altogether. However, there is now lack of clarity among companies in the food business on what they must do with non-standardised food products. Even where standards for food product exist, they often do not comply with international standards causing barriers to imports and exports. On the safety front, there is a lack of testing laboratories and trained officers to test the safety of products. All these have made the process very cumbersome and difficult for companies in the food business.

> The FSSAI's advisories on product approval for non-standardised food products have been arbitrary and changed frequently. The Supreme Court in its order dated August 19, 2015, had declared these advisories as "being arbitrary and hence illegal".

In India, the consumer awareness is low. First, consumers are not aware of the benefits of consuming adequate portions of fruits and vegetables; hardly any steps have been taken by the government to promote such awareness. Second, consumer protection regulations are outdated, consumer courts take time and consumer fora are not strong enough to raise their voices against bad quality produce or to create awareness regarding the benefits of consuming fruits and vegetables.

Further, shortfalls in phytonutrient consumption are usually made up for by nutraceutical supplements in developed countries. In India, however, several factors inhibit the consumption of nutraceuticals. Indian consumers do not supplement their low intake of fruits and vegetables through nutritional supplements. While they may not be aware of this, India does not have any specific regulations for nutraceutical products and food supplements. These are covered under the FSSA, 2006, but the coverage of nutraceuticals remains a somewhat grey area under this Act. There is considerable debate on whether nutraceuticals are curative or preventive,[16] how consumers should access them—i.e., through pharmacy or any other store and/or non-store retail formats—and what the product approval process should be. The FSSAI has proposed a draft Food Safety and Standards (*Food or Health Supplements, Nutraceuticals, Foods for Special Dietary Uses, Foods for Special Medical Purpose, Functional Foods, and Novel Food*) Regulations, 2015.[17] This regulation aims to establish norms for the nutraceutical industry and remove the need to go through a product approval process.[18]

The Indian consumer protection regulation also does not cover issues such as a cooling-off period,[19] which is crucial in the case of sale through non-store formats such as direct selling. The Act also cannot protect consumers against the use of pesticides or insecticides by farmers as the present food supply and the food safety related regulation lacks complete traceability to the farmers. The consumer can however, raise complaints against retailers and manufacturers.

15. See *http://smartinvestor.business-standard.com/market/story-350790-storydet-Food_safety_regulator_and_industry_at_loggerheads_again.htm* (accessed on 6 January 2016)

16. *http://foodsafetyhelpline.com/2014/09/nutraceuticals-challenges-fast-growing-sector-india/* (accessed on 9 December 2015).

17. For detail see *http://www.fssai.gov.in/Portals/0/Pdf/Draft_Notification_Food_Suppliment.pdf* (accessed on 27 November 2015).

18. *http://foodsafetyhelpline.com/2015/07/fssai-proposes-draft-regulations-for-nutraceuticals-functional-foods-and-health-supplements/* (accessed on 9 December 2015).

19. Cooling-off period defines a time frame wherein the customer to withdraw the order within a specified period of time.

6

Summary and Policy Recommendations

India is among the top producers of fruits and vegetables in the world and the country is on a high growth trajectory. The rising middle-class in cities and higher living standards have enabled consumers to shift their spending from essential to discretionary consumption. Despite the changes in spending patterns, food accounts for a major share in consumer spending. However, the share of fruits and vegetables in the consumption basket is low and the consumption patterns is skewed towards cereals. Given this background, this report examines the actual intake of fruits and vegetables by Indian urban upper and middle income consumers and compares it with the WHO recommended quantity of consumption of at least 400 grams of fruits and vegetables (or 5 servings of 80 grams each) per day. The study is based on a primary survey of consumers and secondary data analysis. The survey showed that on an average Indian upper and middle income consumers in metro cities consume 3.5 servings of fruits and vegetables per day and there are variations across income groups, age groups, cities and diet types.

The report further highlights a number of reasons for the shortfall in the intake of fruits and vegetables. These include both supply side and demand side factors. On the supply side, low productivity of fruits and vegetables, restrictions on trade, fragmentation and wastage in the supply chain, poor quality of produce, poor storage and transport infrastructure, lack of quality control at the farm level, barriers to direct sourcing and inter-state mobility have been identified as some of the reasons that prevent the establishment of an efficient supply chain. Production of fruits and vegetables is seasonal and unless the supply chain is efficient there will be wastages, sporadic shortages and price inflation that adversely impact consumers' access to and consumption of fruits and vegetables.

The survey showed that on the demand side, busy lifestyle, lack of options (such as chopped, juices, frozen, etc.) in terms of the forms in which the product can be purchased and consumed, high prices, and concerns related to adulterated fruits and vegetables have led to low consumption. Moreover, a majority of the consumers are not aware of the WHO recommended daily requirements. They are, however, aware of the benefits of fruits and vegetables consumption. In spite of the shortfall in consumption of fruits and vegetables, most Indians do not take health and nutritional supplements.

Whatever may be the reasons for low consumption of fruits and vegetables, it is important to understand that the consumption of fruits and vegetables is essential for maintaining and improving the health of Indians. The concerns are even greater when one looks at the shortfall in consumption for the young Indian and student population, which will contribute to the future workforce. India's strength lies in its large and young population and this group has to remain healthy.

The report highlights a number of regulatory issues related to the APMC Act, FSSA, 2006, and consumer protection regulations, which, if rectified, could support an efficient supply chain, help to increase consumption of fruits and vegetables and protect the interest of consumers. In this context, it is important to note that unlike developed countries, government policies in India have largely ignored the consumers. The focus of the policy has been to protect the interest of farmers, small producers and unorganised retailers. Consumers participating in the survey raised concerns about the quality of fresh and processed fruits and vegetables. Specifically, they referred to the fact that the FSSA, 2006, does not apply to farmers and there are hardly any quality checks on the type of insecticides and pesticides used at the farm level. Further, the process of quality checks is not uniform across states. During the survey, consumers pointed out that the traceability should be to the farm level for food safety. Stringent regulations should ensure that fresh fruits and vegetables meet the desired standards and quality. There should be a system to monitor adulterated products and stringent punishment should be imposed for any malpractices. There should be state-of-the-art testing laboratories for fresh produce and regular checks should be carried out at the *mandis*, local markets, street vendors, etc., to ensure good quality of produce.

In addition, consumer rights are weak and current regulations do not protect the consumers against the use of pesticides at the farm level or adulterated produce. Further, the consumer protection regulation does not comprehensively cover purchases from various stores and non-store retail formats. Hence, this regulation needs to be strengthened/amended to protect consumer interests.

Further, the survey showed that awareness among consumers about food safety and consumer protection is very low. It is the role of the government to create such awareness. The Ministry of Food

Processing Industries and the Ministry of Agriculture & Farmers Welfare should raise awareness through consumer campaigns targeted at raising awareness about the benefits of consuming fruits and vegetables in different forms (cut, salad, cooked, juice, frozen, etc.). Since the young population is more likely to fall short of the WHO recommended intake, it is important for the government to create awareness in schools and colleges. Corporates can be encouraged to use their corporate social responsibility (CSR) funds to support the government in this initiative. During the survey, consumers said that they would like to get such information through print and electronic media. They also pointed out that such information should be made available in local languages and can be displayed in places like local markets where people regularly shop for fruits and vegetables.

It is important to work with farmers and support them by providing training and knowledge sharing to ensure that they use scientific farming techniques that focus on the quality of the produce. The government needs to work closely with private sector and farmers' organisations to provide farmers with right technologies and extension services. Besides, small and mid-sized farmers need help and guidance about the type of pesticides and fertilisers that should be used so that it is not harmful for consumption.

It is a cause for concern that export rejects are sold at a low price in the domestic market, adversely affecting the health of consumers. The Ministry of Health & Family Welfare should set up a committee with the Ministry of Agriculture & Farmers Welfare and the Ministry of Food Processing Industries to address such issues.

In India, consumers show a preference for organic produce and this should be supported by the right policy. Recently, the government has liberalised foreign investment in horticulture, cultivation of vegetables and mushroom and agro and allied sectors. This is a step in the right direction as it may help to bring in global best practices. However, foreign investors will not be able to work at the farm level if other regulatory issues, such as restrictions on contract farming, are not addressed. It is also important to monitor private and foreign investment so that the interests of farmers, producers and consumers are protected.

To increase availability and choice, the government may explore the possibilities of liberalising FDI in multi-brand retail. Rigid conditions in FDI regulations should be removed and the consumers should have the freedom to select the mode of purchase (store or non-store retail format, Indian or foreign retailer), and form of purchase (branded or unbranded, organic or non-organic). They should have access to a variety of products.

At present, there are restrictions on imports of fruits and vegetables through high tariffs and other barriers. However, this report shows that tariffs on a number of items will be lowered in a phased manner under trade agreements such as the India-ASEAN FTA. This is likely to benefit consumers in terms of wider access and choices. Barriers to imports of key products such as onions contribute to price rise. Such import restrictions should be removed. Imports should be allowed to match shortfalls in domestic production.

Like all countries, India has seasonal production of fruits and vegetables. However, in other countries, shortages of fruits and vegetables are met through imports, efficient storage facilities and processing. In India, the level of processing is low. Although the government has come up with a number of schemes such as the Mega Food Park scheme to set up food parks, benefits are not given to food processors or units under such grant-based schemes. Therefore, food processors are not keen to locate units in such parks, unless park developers themselves have captive units. The government can encourage food processing through right policies targeted at food processors. Incentives should be linked to performance. Further, government can help food processors by sharing information on quality, by working with the private sector to have state-of-the-art product testing laboratories, etc. Lower taxes on processed fruits and vegetables will increase consumption.

The government should identify gaps in food supply chain infrastructure and policy should focus on creation of the right infrastructure. For example, there is a shortage of pack houses in India and subsidies may be directed to pack houses instead of cold storages. Further, the cost of electricity is high and the supply is erratic, which make pack houses non-viable. Often private pack houses and cold storages charge high rates for storage, which are unaffordable for small and mid-sized farmers. Further, there are hardly any cold storage facilities in agricultural markets or *mandis*. These infrastructure bottlenecks have to be addressed through right

Ensure traceability back to the farm to ensure maintenance of hygiene and quality standards	Work with farmers, support their training and share knowledge	Cover both store and non-store retail formats under consumer protection regulations
Generate awareness among consumers, especially students and the younger cohort regarding the recommended intake of fruits and vegetables	Ministry of Food Processing Industries should generate awareness about the benefits of processed fruits and vegetables	Improve availability of organic products
Restrictions on contract farming should be addressed to attract investments at the farm level	Private investments should be monitored to safeguard the interests of farmers, producers and consumers	Performance linked incentives should be given to food processors to encourage food processing
Government can help food processors by sharing information on quality, working with the private sector to have state-of-the-art product testing laboratories, etc.	Lower taxes on processed fruits and vegetables	Government may explore the possibility of liberalising FDI in multi-brand retail and ease conditions on foreign investors to improve access to a variety of products
Identify gaps in food supply chain infrastructure and focus policy on the creation of the right infrastructure	Infrastructure bottlenecks have to be addressed through right policies	Delist fruits and vegetables from APMC so that there is no APMC cess and remove restrictions on inter-state movement of fruits and vegetables

policies. Instead of giving subsidies for sporadic development of infrastructure, subsidies should address the gaps in the food supply chain. State government could consider providing electricity at lower rates to pack houses. If a pack house or cold storage is created on government subsidy, it has to offer its services to small and mid-sized farmers at subsidised rates. The government can delist fruits and vegetables from APMC so that there is no APMC cess. There should not be any restrictions on inter-state movement of fruits and vegetables. Further, wastage can be reduced through a green channel[1] so that trucks for perishable products like fruits and vegetables do not have to stop at inter-state check points and can move faster.

Overall, the policy focus should be on lower and stable prices for fruits and vegetables, which can

1. Green channel is a dedicated network for transport. Under this system, payments are made online and by producing the receipt at the check-post, trucks can pass through inter-state check posts without queuing for payment of taxes. This leads to faster movement of trucks.

be achieved by improving supply chain efficiency, reducing the number of intermediaries, reducing wastage, reducing restrictions on imports and ensuring the quality of produce. The focus of the government should also be to support farmers to improve productivity and to produce products of a quality that can be processed and exported. Protection of consumer health should be a key point in policymaking.

A key concern, which came up during the survey, was that consumers are not too aware of nutritional supplements. Besides, the policy related to nutritional and food supplements is still evolving. The FSSAI should come up with a comprehensive policy where consumers have access to nutritional supplements through various store and non-store retail formats.

Last but not least, to remain healthy, Indians should have the desired quantity of fruits and vegetables in their daily diet. While consumption decisions are personal, the government, through appropriate policy, awareness programmes, etc., can support the desired consumption of fruits and vegetables which, in turn, will help to have a healthy nation. Most importantly, government policy has to protect the interests of consumers and provide them with a broader choice in terms of purchase decisions and product variety.

References

Aiyer, H.S., S. Kichambare and R.C. Gupta (2008). "Prevention of Oxidative DNA Damage by Bioactive Berry Components", *Nutrition and Cancer* 60(1): 36 42.

Beecher, G.R. (1999). "Phytonutrients' Role in Metabolism: Effects on Resistance to Degenerative Processes", *Nutrition Review* 57(9): S3–S6, September.

Bhattacharya, Rudrani and Abhijeet Sen Gupta (2015). "Food Inflation in India: Causes and Consequences", *Working Paper* No. 2015-151. New Delhi: National Institute of Public Finance and Policy. Available at *http://www.nipfp.org.in/media/medialibrary/2015/07/WP_2015_151.pdf* (accessed on 22 July 2015).

Central Institute of Post Harvest Engineering & Technology (CIPHET) (2013). *Vision 2050*. Ludhiana. *http://ciphet.in/upload/file/Vision_2050%20revised%20on_6-7_13.pdf* (accessed on 22 July 2015).

Credit Suisse (2015). *Global Wealth Report 2015*. Switzerland: Credit Suisse, Research Institute, October. Available at *https://publications.credit-suisse.com/tasks/render/file/?fileID=F2425415-DCA7-80B8-EAD989AF9341D47E* (accessed on 7 December 2015).

Department of Scientific and Industrial Research (2010). *Technology Export Potential Reports "Fruits and Vegetable Sector: An Overview"*. New Delhi: International Technology Transfer Programme. Available at *http://dsir.gov.in/reports/ittp_tedo/agro/AF_Farm_Fruits_Vegetables_Intro.pdf* (accessed on 22 July 2015).

Eapen, Leena Mary and Sthanu R. Nair (2012). "Food Price Inflation in India (2008 to 2010)", *Economic and Political Weekly* XLVII (20), 19 May.

Food and Agriculture Organization of the United Nations (FAO) (2012). *The State of Food and Agriculture: Investing in Food and Agriculture for a Better Future*. Rome, Italy. Available at *http://www.fao.org/docrep/017/i3028e/i3028e.pdf* (accessed on 7 December 2015).

————. (2015). *Definition and Classification of Commodities*. Rome, Italy. Available at *http://www.fao.org/es/faodef/faodefe.htm* (accessed on 22 July 2015).

Garcia-Lafuente, A., E. Guillamon, A. Villares, M.A. Rostagno and J.A. Martinez (2009). "Flavonoids as Anti-inflammatory Agents: Implications in Cancer and Cardiovascular Disease", *Inflammation Research* 58(9): 537-52.

Gillman M.W., L.A. Cupples, D. Gagnon, B.M. Posner, R.C. Ellison, W.P. Castelli and P.A. Wolf (1995). "Protective Effect of Fruits and Vegetables on Development of Stroke in Men" *Journal of the American Medical Association* 273(14): 1113-17.

Images Multimedia Private Limited (2015). *India Retail Report 2015*. New Delhi.

International Monetary Fund (IMF) (2015). *World Economic Outlook: Country and Regional Perspectives*. Washington, D.C. Available at *http://www.imf.org/external/pubs/ft/weo/2015/01/pdf/c2.pdf* (accessed on 22 July 2015).

Joseph, J.A., B. Shukitt-Hale and L.M. Willis (2009). "Grape Juice, Berries, and Walnuts Affect Brain Aging and Behavior", *Journal of Nutrition* 139(9): 1813S-17S.

Khan, N, V.M. Adhami and H. Mukhtar (2010). "Apoptosis by Dietary Agents for Prevention and Treatment of Prostate Cancer", *Endocrine-Related Cancer* 17(1): R39-R52.

Lee, H.S., Y.H. Cho, J. Park, H.R. Shin, and J.M.K. Sung (2013). "Dietary Intake of Phytonutrients in Relation to Fruit and Vegetable Consumption in Korea", *Journal of the Academy of Nutrition and Dietetics* 113(9): 1194-99.

Liu, R.H. (2013). "Health-promoting Components of Fruits and Vegetables in the Diet", *Advances in Nutrition* 4(3): 384S–92S.

McKinsey & Company (2007). *The Bird of Gold: The Rise of India's Consumer Market*. McKinsey Global Institute, India. Available at *http://www.mckinsey.com/insights/asia pacific/the_bird_of_gold* (accessed on 22 July 2015).

Mente, A., L. de Koning, H.S. Shannon and S.S. Anand (2009). "A Systematic Review of the Evidence Supporting a Causal Link Between Dietary Factors and Coronary Heart Disease", *Journal of the American Medical Association, Internal Medicine* 169(7): 659-69.

Morand, C., C. Dubray, D. Milenkovic, D. Lioger, J.F. Martin, A. Scalbert and A. Mazur (2011). "Hesperidin Contributes to the Vascular Protective Effects of Orange Juice: A Randomized Crossover Study in Healthy Volunteers", *The American Journal of Clinical Nutrition* 93(1): 73-80.

Mukherjee, A., T. M. Goyal, P. Pal and S. Deb (2014). *Food Supply Chain in India: Analysing the Potential for International Business*. New Delhi: Academic Foundation.

Murphy, M.M., Leila M. Barraj, Judith H. Spungen, Dena R. Herman and R. Keith Randolph (2012). "Phytonutrient Intake by Adults in the United States in Relation to Fruit and Vegetable Consumption", *Journal of the Academy of Nutrition and Dietetics*, 112(2): 222-29, February.

————. (2014). "Global Assessment of Select Phytonutrient Intakes by Level of Fruit and Vegetable Consumption", *British Journal of Nutrition* 112(6): 1004-18.

National Centre for Cold Chain Development (NCCD) and National Bank for Agricultural and Rural Development (NABARD) Consultancy Service (2015). *All India Cold-chain Infrastructure Capacity: Assessment of Status & Gap*. NCCD and Nabcon. Available at *http://www.nccd.gov.in/PDF/CCSG_Final%20Report_Web.pdf* (accessed on 9 December 2015).

National Horticulture Board (2014). *Indian Horticulture Database 2014*. New Delhi: Ministry of Agriculture, Government of India. Available at *http://www.nhb.gov.in/area-pro/NHB_Database_2015.pdf* (accessed on 22 July 2015).

National Institute of Medical Statistics, Indian Council of Medical Research (ICMR) (2009). *IDSP Non-Communicable Disease Risk Factors Survey, Phase-I States of India, 2007-08*. New Delhi: Government of India. Available at *http://www.icmr.nic.in/final/IDSP-NCD%20Reports/Phase-1%20States%20of%20India.pdf* (accessed on 22 July 2015).

National Council of Applied Economic Research (NCAER) (2014). *Agricultural Outlook and Situation Analysis Report: An Analysis of Changing Food Consumption Pattern in India*. New Delhi. pp.9-15.

National Sample Survey Organisation (NSSO) (2014). *Household Consumer Expenditure, NSS 50th-68th Round Reports*. New Delhi: Ministry of Statistics and Programme Implementation. Available at *http://mail.mospi.gov.in/index.php/catalog/?sort_by=proddate&sort_order=asc&* (accessed on 25 July 2015).

Nutrilite Health Institute (2014). *Global Phytonutrient Report*. California, US: Center for Optimal Health.

Nutrilite Health Institute (2015). *The Shortfall of Fruits, Vegetable and Phytonutrient Consumption in Asia with a Focus on India*. California, US: Center for Optimal Health.

Olson, J.H., J.C. Erie, S.J. Bakri (2011). "Nutritional Supplementation and Age Related Macular Degeneration", *Seminars in Ophthalmology* 26(3): 131-36.

Planning Commission (2012). *The Committee on Encouraging Investments in Supply Chains Including Provision for Cold Storages for More Efficient Distribution of Farm Produce*. New Delhi, India. Available at *http://planningcommission.gov.in/reports/genrep/rep_supply1312.pdf* (accessed on 25 July 2015)

Shukla, R. (2010). *How India Earns, Spends and Saves: Unmasking the Real India*. New Delhi: Sage Publications India Private Limited and NCAER.

Son, Y.O., S.H. Kook, K.C. Choi, Y.S. Jang, Y.S. Choi, Y.M. Jeon, J.G. Kim, H.S. Hwang and J.C. Lee (2008). "Quercetin Accelerates TNF-alpha Induced Apoptosis of MC3T3-E1 Osteoblastic Cells through Caspase Dependent and JNK-mediated Pathways", *European Journal of Pharmacology* 579(1-3): 26-33.

Steinmetz, K.A. and J.D. Potter (1996). "Vegetable, Fruits and Cancer Prevention: A Review", *Journal of the American Dietetic Association* 96(10): 1027-39.

The Boston Consulting Group (2012). *The Tiger Roars: An In-depth Analysis of How a Billion Plus People Consume. India*. Available at *http://www.indiaretailing.com/upload/ContentImage/Market_Research_pdf/The_Tiger_Roars.pdf* (accessed on 25 July 2015).

World Health Organization (WHO) (2003). "Health System Performance Assessment, World Health Survey (2003)", *Wave O, India*. ID NO,: IND_2003_WHS_v01_M. Available at *http://www.who.int/healthinfo/survey/whsind-india.pdf* (accessed on 25 July 2015).

WHO/FAO (2003). "Diet, Nutrition, and the Prevention of Chronic Diseases", *TRS* no. 916. Geneva. Available at *http://whqlibdoc.who.int/trs/who_trs_916.pdf* (accessed on 25 July 2015).

Yes Bank Limited and Ministry of Food Processing Industries (2014). *Fruits and Vegetables Availability Maps of India*. Food and Agribusiness Strategic Advisory & Research (FASAR), Yes Bank Limited and Ministry of Food Processing Industries. December. Available at *http://mofpi.nic.in/H_Dwld.aspx?KYEwmOL+HGqTV0f1VSVZLW3VlDC+YHsvTxu0wQ5UZV5yHmWs6HjdrQ==* (accessed on 29 January 2016)

Appendices

Appendix A

Production, Export and Import Trends of Select Fruits and Vegetables

Table A.1: Fruit Area, Production and Productivity—All India (2001-02 to 2013-14)

Year	Fruit Area ('000 HA)	Fruit Production ('000 MT)	Fruit Productivity (MT/HA)	Year-on-Year (YoY) Productivity
2001-02	4,010	43,001	10.72	
2002-03	3,788	45,203	11.93	0.113
2003-04	4,661	45,942	9.86	-0.174
2004-05	5,049	50,867	10.07	0.022
2005-06	5,324	55,356	10.40	0.032
2006-07	5,554	59,563	10.72	0.031
2007-08	5,857	65,587	11.20	0.044
2008-09	6,101	68,466	11.22	0.002
2009-10	6,329	71,516	11.30	0.007
2010-11	6,383	74,878	11.73	0.038
2011-12	6,705	76,424	11.40	-0.028
2012-13	6,982	81,285	11.64	0.021
2013-14	7,216	88,977	12.33	0.059

Source: Compiled from National Horticulture Board (2014), Page 2, Table titled: "Indian Horticulture Production at a Glance". Available at: *http://www.nhb.gov.in/area-pro/NHB_Database_2015.pdf* (accessed on 30 November 2015).

Table A.2: Vegetable Area, Production and Productivity—All India (2001-02 to 2013-14)

Year	Vegetable Area ('000 HA)	Vegetable Production ('000 MT)	Vegetable Productivity (MT/HA)	YoY Productivity
2001-02	6,156	88,622	14.40	-
2002-03	6,092	84,815	13.92	-0.033
2003-04	6,082	88,334	14.52	0.043
2004-05	6,744	1,01,246	15.01	0.034
2005-06	7,213	1,11,399	15.44	0.029
2006-07	7,581	1,14,993	15.17	-0.018
2007-08	7,848	1,28,449	16.37	0.079
2008-09	7,981	1,29,077	16.17	-0.012
2009-10	7,985	1,33,738	16.75	0.036
2010-11	8,495	1,46,554	17.25	0.030
2011-12	8,989	1,56,325	17.39	0.008
2012-13	9,205	1,62,187	17.62	0.013
2013-14	9,396	1,62,897	17.34	-0.016

Source: Compiled from National Horticulture Board (2014), Page 2, Table titled: "Indian Horticulture Production at a Glance". Available *at: http://www.nhb.gov.in/area-pro/NHB_Database_2015.pdf* (accessed on 30 November 2015).

Table A.3: Select Fruits Availability—All India (2001-02 to 2013-14)

Year	Banana Area ('000 HA)	Mango Area ('000 HA)	Banana Production ('000 MT)	Mango Production ('000 MT)	Banana Export (MT)	Mango Export (MT)	Banana Import (MT)	Mango Import (MT)
2001-02	466	1,576	14,210	10,020	8,100	44,802	N.A	0
2002-03	475	1,623	13,304	12,733	8,656	38,238	6	56
2003-04	499	1,907	13,857	11,490	10,877	162,045	N.A	48
2004-05	590	1,970	16,745	11,830	12,818	153,345	N.A	38
2005-06	570	2,081	18,888	12,663	14,411	207,255	N.A	14
2006-07	604	2,154	20,998	13,734	11,476	238,887	3	42
2007-08	658	2,201	23,823	13,997	16,663	226,148	N.A	76
2008-09	709	2,309	26,217	12,750	30,402	258,216	N.A	31
2009-10	770	2,312	26,470	15,027	54,273	264,726	0	216
2010-11	830	2,297	29,780	15,188	57,539	230,112	1	91
2011-12	797	2,378	28,455	16,196	45,582	219,422	N.A	14
2012-13	776	2,500	26,509	18,002	50,004	205,666	N.A	13
2013-14	803	2,516	29,725	18,431	36,256	182,850	4	41

Note: HS: Codes are 0803 (Banana) and 08045020-40 (Mango including sliced, dried and pulp). Codes were revised after April 2013. N.A: not available.

Source: Compiled from the National Horticulture Database 2014 (Available at: *http://nhb.gov.in/area-pro/NHB_Database_2015.pdf*) and Export Import Data Bank, Ministry of Commerce (Accessible at: *http://dgft.gov.in/*) (Accessed on 22 November 2015).

Table A.4: Select Vegetables Availability—All India (2001-02 to 2013-14)

Year	Onion Area ('000 HA)	Tomato Area ('000 HA)	Onion Production ('000 MT)	Tomato Production ('000 MT)	Onion Export (MT)	Tomato Export (MT)	Onion Import (MT)	Tomato Import (MT)
2001-02	496	458	5,252	7,462	441,849.59	1,413	N.A	N.A
2002-03	425	479	4,210	7,617	588,711.75	12,886	0	N.A
2003-04	554	503	6,268	8,126	859,939	11,328	N.A	32
2004-05	614	505	7,761	8,825	870,217	7,446	0	5
2005-06	704	546	9,433	9,820	960,507	11,743	6,570	51
2006-07	768	596	10,847	10,055	1,378,373	33,593	N.A	41
2007-08	821	566	13,900	10,303	1,008,606	134,845	104	33
2008-09	834	599	13,565	11,149	1,670,186	124,617	89	62
2009-10	756	634	12,159	12,433	1,676,562	105,557	630	42
2010-11	1,064	865	15,118	16,826	1,182,324	65,872	12,506	63
2011-12	1,087	907	17,511	18,653	1,309,925	266,986	13	N.A
2012-13	1,052	880	16,813	18,227	1,666,873	343,692	450	2
2013-14	1,204	882	19,402	18,736	1,402,606	399,838	17,847	4

Note: HS: Codes 07031010 (Onion) and 07020000 (Tomato) for selected commodities. N.A: not available.

Source: Compiled from the National Horticulture Database 2014 (Available at: *http://nhb.gov.in/area-pro/NHB_Database_2015.pdf) and Export Import Data Bank, Ministry of Commerce. (Accessible at: http://dgft.gov.in/)* (Accessed on 22 November 2015).

Appendix B

Prices of Select Commodities across Different Centres in India

Table B.1: Wholesale Price, Retail Price and Total Arrival of Tomato 2014

Tomato	*January*			*April*			*July*			*October*		
Centre Name	*WAP*	*RAP*	*TA*	*WAP*	*RAP*	*TA*	*WAP*	*RAP*	*TA*	*WAP*	*RAP*	*TA*
Chandigarh	1,656	2,688	1,057	1,350	2,280	816	1,640	2,708	1,085	2,045	3,455	992
Chennai	736	1,196	2,570	1,302	1,945	1,310	3,708	4,562	1,970	1,254	1,861	1,715
Delhi	1,169	2,323	17,937	1,093	2,109	13,213	1,147	2,380	7,381	1,689	3,652	10,531
Hyderabad	0	0	0	0	0	0	0	0	0	729	1,233	1,005
Kolkata	1,318	1,938	2,745	1,160	1,917	513	4,269	6,152	2,370	2,485	4,174	2,160
Lucknow	0	0	0	0	0	0	4,495	5,946	874	2,389	3,036	1,386
Mumbai	942	1,550	7,627	991	1,341	6,213	4,085	5,442	6,089	1,636	2,273	7,614

Note: WAP: Wholesale Average Price (in INR/Qtl); RAP: Retail Average Price (in INR/Qtl); TA: Total Arrival (in MT).

Source: Extracted from the NHB website *http://nhb.gov.in/OnlineClient/MonthwiseAnnualPriceandArrivalReport.aspx?enc=3ZOO8K5CzcdC/Yq6HcdIxJ4o5jmAcGG5QGUXX3BIAP4=* (Accessed on 30 November 2015).

Table B.2: Wholesale Price, Retail Price and Total Arrival of Onion 2014

Onion	*January*			*April*			*July*			*October*		
Centre Name	*WAP*	*RAP*	*TA*	*WAP*	*RAP*	*TA*	*WAP*	*RAP*	*TA*	*WAP*	*RAP*	*TA*
Chandigarh	1,291	2,024	1,677	1,124	1,825	1,472	1,727	2,735	1,767	1,715	2,509	1,344
Chennai	1,471	2,371	16,510	1323	1,900	10,590	2,988	3,785	12,880	2,335	2,948	10,610
Delhi	1,274	2,196	21,078	1,232	1,827	22,407	2,040	3,035	22,440	1,751	3,091	21,645
Hyderabad	844	1,428	8,999	547	872	7,195	1,360	2,110	6,877	1,821	2,465	3,391
Kolkata	1,488	2,444	45,160	1,110	1,857	4,445	2,509	3,507	14,992	2,071	3,200	10,160
Lucknow	1,348	1,737	696	1,253	1,889	2,000	1,932	2,638	1,536	1,841	2,236	1,375
Mumbai	1,140	1,952	26,140	952	1,614	22,546	2,178	2,923	18,305	1,562	2,310	17,365

Note: WAP: Wholesale Average Price (in INR/Qtl); RAP: Retail Average Price (in INR/Qtl); TA: Total Arrival (in MT).

Source: Extracted from the NHB website *http://nhb.gov.in/OnlineClient/MonthwiseAnnualPriceandArrivalReport.aspx?enc=3ZOO8K5CzcdC/Yq6HcdIxJ4o5jmAcGG5QGUXX3BIAP4=* (Accessed on 30 November 2015).

Table B.3: Wholesale Price, Retail Price and Total Arrival of Cauliflower—January-December 2014

Cauliflower	*January*			*April*			*July*			*October*		
Center Name	*WAP*	*RAP*	*TA*	*WAP*	*RAP*	*TA*	*WAP*	*RAP*	*TA*	*WAP*	*RAP*	*TA*
Chandigarh	528	952	1,541	767	1,385	625	0	0	0	2,196	3,532	557
Chennai	1,758	2,625	1,798	1,982	2,864	1,127	3,396	4,746	903	2,817	4,021	1,242
Delhi	685	1,485	4,569	582	1,550	2,720	2,268	4,200	3,949	1,279	3,600	5,146
Hyderabad	828	1,356	1,117	783	1,361	1,065	1,695	2,435	825	1,109	1,794	972
Kolkata	1,104	1,529	2,802	1,711	2,615	119	2,483	3,688	354	2,359	3,796	891
Lucknow	358	570	2,842	878	1,525	37	0	0	0	2,272	2,991	1,248
Mumbai	681	2,346	6,039	657	1,282	3,568	1,738	4,000	12,014	1,273	2,700	3,550

Note: WAP: Wholesale Average Price (in INR/Qtl); RAP: Retail Average Price (in INR/Qtl); TA: Total Arrival (in MT).

Source: Extracted from the NHB website *http://nhb.gov.in/OnlineClient/MonthwiseAnnualPriceandArrivalReport.aspx?enc=3ZOO8K5CzcdC/Yq6HcdIxJ4o5jmAcGG5QGUXX3BIAP4=* (accessed on 30 November 2015).

Table B.4: Wholesale Price, Retail Price and Total Arrival of Okra—January-December 2014

Okra	*January*			*April*			*July*			*October*		
Centre Name	WAP	RAP	TA	WAP	RAP	TA	WAP	RAP	TA	WAP	RAP	TA
Chandigarh	0	0	0	0	0	0	1,722	3,119	1,123	2,682	3,891	229
Chennai	2,225	2,996	496	1,636	2,473	624	2,662	4,954	591	1,442	2,142	779
Delhi	3,705	4,346	1,843	3,309	5,418	3,515	1,574	2,508	3,400	1,727	3,009	920
Hyderabad	1,008	1,500	866	1,256	1,939	878	1,560	2,200	849	1,918	2,665	1,025
Kolkata	0	0	0	1,851	2,809	188	2,129	3,162	278	2,651	4,043	114
Lucknow	1,100	1,400	60	2,383	3,568	413	1,227	1,873	581	1,424	2,159	200
Mumbai	2,654	4,154	3,090	2,141	3,295	4,017	2,656	4,346	2,395	1,773	3,136	2,814

Note: WAP: Wholesale Average Price (in INR/Qtl); RAP: Retail Average Price (in INR/Qtl); TA: Total Arrival (in MT).

Source: Extracted from the NHB website *http://nhb.gov.in/OnlineClient/MonthwiseAnnualPriceandArrivalReport.aspx?enc=3ZOO8K5CzcdC/Yq6HcdlxJ4o5jmAcGG5QGUXX3BlAP4=* (accessed on 30 November 2015).

Table B.5: Wholesale Price, Retail Price and Total Arrival of Banana—January-December 2014

Banana	*January*			*April*			*July*			*October*		
Centre Name	WAP	RAP	TA	WAP	RAP	TA	WAP	RAP	TA	WAP	RAP	TA
Chandigarh	2,211	3,700	821	3,101	5,076	814	2,545	4,296	1,106	2,596	4,418	982
Chennai	2,180	3,028	2,580	2,177	3,073	1,775	2,162	3,062	2,270	2,083	2,991	1,935
Delhi	1,694	2,077	2,366	1,665	2,300	4,368	1,354	1,856	8,307	1,542	1,810	5,681
Hyderabad	2,004	2,708	1,362	2,130	2,745	1,659	2,309	2,857	3,299	2,344	3,341	3,334
Kolkata	1,138	2,192	1,950	1,606	2,861	1,792	1,364	2,327	3,936	1,373	2,414	2,392
Lucknow	973	1,758	1,695	1,057	2,614	14,695	1,263	2,504	1,741	1,120	2,140	1,916
Mumbai	1,229	2,173	650	1,920	2,659	291	1,810	2,808	359	1,882	2,682	341

Note: WAP: Wholesale Average Price (in INR/Qtl); RAP: Retail Average Price (in INR/Qtl); TA: Total Arrival (in MT).

Source: Extracted from the NHB website *http://nhb.gov.in/OnlineClient/MonthwiseAnnualPriceandArrivalReport.aspx?enc=3ZOO8K5CzcdC/Yq6HcdlxJ4o5jmAcGG5QGUXX3BlAP4=* (accessed on 30 November 2015).

Table B.6: Wholesale Price, Retail Price and Total Arrival of Mango (Dussehri)—January-December 2014

Mango	*January*			*April*			*July*			*October*		
Centre Name	WAP	RAP	TA	WAP	RAP	TA	WAP	RAP	TA	WAP	RAP	TA
Chandigarh	0	0	0	0	0	0	2,331	3,685	1,204	0	0	0
Chennai	0	0	0	0	0	0	6,565	8,346	186	0	0	0
Delhi	0	0	0	3,547	5,321	11,808	3,074	4,981	78,777	0	0	0
Kolkata	0	0	0	0	0	0	3,403	5,330	3,648	0	0	0
Lucknow	0	0	0	0	0	0	2,182	3,435	6,631	0	0	0
Mumbai	1,700	3,000	221	0	0	0	3,738	4,820	0	0	0	0

Note: WAP: Wholesale Average Price (in INR/Qtl); RAP: Retail Average Price (in INR/Qtl); TA: Total Arrival (in MT).

Source: Extracted from the NHB website *http://nhb.gov.in/OnlineClient/MonthwiseAnnualPriceandArrivalReport.aspx?enc=3ZOO8K5CzcdC/Yq6HcdlxJ4o5jmAcGG5QGUXX3BlAP4=* (accessed on 30 November 2015).

Table B.7: Wholesale Price, Retail Price and Total Arrival of Orange—January-December 2014

Orange	*January*			*April*			*July*			*October*		
Centre Name	WAP	RAP	TA	WAP	RAP	TA	WAP	RAP	TA	WAP	RAP	TA
Chandigarh	2,766	4,415	606	3,451	6,025	661	0	0	0	2,977	4,877	663
Chennai	3,525	5,000	759	0	0	0	0	0	0	3,300	5,000	40
Delhi	3,579	5,231	3,417	5,608	6,773	1,153	0	0	0	3,895	5,878	4,362
Hyderabad	0	0	0	0	0	0	0	0	0	0	0	0
Kolkata	2,898	4,073	2,720	4,855	6,809	464	0	0	0	3,041	4,400	1,120
Lucknow	2,865	3,996	344	3,959	6,532	501	0	0	0	0	0	0
Mumbai	1,589	2,818	1,982	2,420	3,477	889	2,227	3,538	1,033	1,991	3,045	3,133

Note: WAP: Wholesale Average Price (in INR/Qtl); RAP: Retail Average Price (in INR/Qtl); TA: Total Arrival (in MT).

Source: Extracted from the NHB website *http://nhb.gov.in/OnlineClient/MonthwiseAnnualPriceandArrivalReport.aspx?enc=3ZOO8K5CzcdC/Yq6HcdlxJ4o5jmAcGG5QGUXX3BlAP4=* (accessed on 30 November 2015).

Appendix C

Consumer Survey Questionnaire

I. About Yourself and Your Family

1. *Personal Details*

a.	Name of the Respondent		
b.	Complete Address (with city and pin code to trace location)		
c.	Fixed Phone (Office)		Mobile No.
d.	E-mail address		
e.	Name of the Interviewer		f. Date of interview

2. *Your Sex:*

Sex	*Male*	*Female*
Please tick the relevant option		

3. *Your Age group:*

Age Group (in years)	*Code*	*Tick as appropriate*
18-25	1	
25-35	2	
35-50	3	
50-60	4	
Above 60	5	

4. *Your Education:*

Education	*Code*	*Tick as appropriate*
Literate but without formal schooling	1	
Schooling (secondary school completed/ high school completed)	2	
Some college but not graduate	3	
Technical Education/Diploma/ Certificate/Vocational	4	
Graduate	5	
Post Graduate (Technical)	6	
Post Graduate (Non- Technical)	7	
Higher Research Degrees	8	
Others, please specify		

Note: Technical education includes degrees like engineering and medical degrees etc. Non-technical will include management degrees/PG diploma etc.

5. *Your Occupation:*

Occupation	*Code*	*Tick as appropriate*
Officer/Executive – Middle/Senior	1	
Officer/Executive – Junior	2	
Supervisory Level	3	
Clerical	4	
Salesman	5	
Entrepreneurs	6	
Shop Owner	7	
Petty Trader	8	
Home makers/Housewives	9	
Students	10	
Pensioners	11	
Others, please specify		

6. *Asset Ownership of your household:*

Item	*Code*	*Tick all appropriate*
Air conditioner	1	
Refrigerator	2	
Washing machine	3	
Two-wheeler	4	
Four-wheeler	5	
LCD/Plasma TV	6	
Debit card	7	
Credit card	8	
Mobile phone	9	
Personal computer	10	
House/property	11	
Others, please specify		
Total		

7. *Tell us about your household composition:*

7.1	About your family		*Tick as appropriate*
		a. Living alone	
		b. Nuclear family	
		c. Joint family	
7.2	Number of members in the household		
7.3	Number of members below the age of 18		
7.4	Number of earning members		
7.5	Relationship with the main income earner		

8. Which income category would your personal annual income and household annual income fall under (we are only considering middle income and above)?

Income Levels (in INR)	*a Personal code*	*Tick as appropriate*	*b Household Code*	*Tick as appropriate*
2 lakhs–5 lakhs	1		1	
5 lakhs–10 lakhs	2		2	
10 lakhs–15 lakhs	3		3	
15 lakhs–25 lakhs	4		4	
Above 25 lakhs	5		5	

8.1 What proportion of your annual household disposable income (income net of taxes) do you spend on the following? (Please indicate in percentage for each category. Note that the total should add up to 100%)

			Percentage (%)
8.1.1	Consumption	a. Fresh and preserved fruits and vegetables	
		b. Apparels	
		c. Accessories (handbags, footwear etc.)	
		d. Jewellery	
		e. Consumer durables	
		Others, please specify ____	
8.1.2	House rent		
8.1.3	Education and health		
8.1.4	Recreational activities and holidays		
8.1.5	Savings and investments		
8.1.6	EMI/loan repayment		
Others, please specify _____			

II. Consumption and Purchase of Fruits and Vegetables

9. Who generally purchases fruits and vegetables for the household?

Purchase Incidence	*Code*	*Tick as appropriate*
Self	1	
Family Members	2	
House help	3	
Others, please specify _____		

10. Where is the shopping for fruits and vegetables generally done?

Source	*Code*	*Tick as appropriate*
Push cart	1	
Other unorganised retail (e.g.,nearby local market)	2	
Organised retail (e.g., Big Bazaar)	3	
Wholesale market ('mandi')	4	
Others, please specify_____		

11. Quantity of fruits and vegetables generally purchased.

11.1 Do you know the quantity of fruits and vegetables purchased by you or by your household?

Tick as appropriate	*Personal*	*Household*	*If No, go to Question 12*
Yes			
No			

11.2 If yes to question 11.1, what quantities of vegetables do you or your household typically purchase weekly and monthly?

Please note that this survey excludes the purchase of potatoes and other starchy tubers such as cassava ('arabi'), sweet potato, etc.

Quantity		*a. Personal Code*	*Tick as appropriate*	*b. Household Code*	*Tick as appropriate*
11.2.1 Weekly	Less than 10 kg	1		1	
	10 kg–15 kg	2		2	
	Above 15 kg	3		3	
11.2.2 Monthly	Less than 20 kg	1		1	
	20 kg–40 kg	2		2	
	Above 40 kg	3		3	

11.3 If yes to question 11.1, what quantities of fruits do you or your household typically purchase weekly and monthly?

Quantity		*a. Personal Code*	*Tick as appropriate*	*b. Household Code*	*Tick as appropriate*
11.3.1 Weekly	Less than 10 kg	1		1	
	10 kg–15 kg	2		2	
	Above 15 kg	3		3	
11.3.2 Monthly	Less than 20 kg	1		1	
	20 kg–40 kg	2		2	
	Above 40 kg	3		3	

12. What is your average weekly and monthly personal and household expenditure on fruits and vegetables excluding potato and other tubers such as cassava ('*arabi*'), sweet potato, and ginger and garlic?

12.1 Weekly Expenditure on fruits and vegetables (in INR)	*a. Personal Code*	*Tick as appropriate*	*b. Household Code*	*Tick as appropriate*
	Less than 1,000		Less than 1,000	
	1,000–2,000		1,000–2,000	
	2,000–3,000		2000–3,000	
	3,000–4,000		3,000–4,000	
	4,000–5,000		4,000–5,000	
	Above 5,000		Above 5,000	
12.2 Monthly Expenditure on fruits and vegetables (in INR)	*a. Personal Code*	*Tick as appropriate*	*b. Household Code*	*Tick as appropriate*
	Less than 5,000		Less than 5,000	
	5,000–8,000		5,000–8,000	
	8,000–10,000		8,000–10,000	
	Above 10,000		Above 10,000	

13. What is the monthly personal and household expenditure on all food items [including cereals, lentils, meat (including fish and chicken), fruits and vegetables, spices, etc.]?

Monthly Expenditure (in INR)	*13.1 Personal Code*	*Tick as appropriate*	*13.2 Household Code*	*Tick as appropriate*
Less than 10,000	1		1	
10,000–30,000	2		2	
30,000– 50,000	3		3	
Above 50,000	4		4	

14. Based on your consumption of fruits and vegetables, egg and/or meat, please answer the following question:

Which of the following best describes your diet?

Diet	*Description*	*Tick as appropriate*
Jain diet	Eat no meat (including fish or chicken), onion, garlic or other vegetables grown underground	
Vegetarian diet	Eat milk and milk products, but no egg and meat (including fish or chicken)	
Eggetarian diet	Eat egg, milk and milk products, but no meat (including fish or chicken)	
Non-vegetarian diet	Eat meat (including fish or chicken)	
Others, please specify	____	

14.1 Do you have any dietary restriction or food allergy?

	Tick as appropriate		
	Yes	No	*If No, skip to Question 15.*
Dietary Restrictions			
Food allergy			

14.2 Does a dietary restriction or food allergy prevent you from consuming any of the following fruits and vegetables?

14.2.1 Vegetables

(Tick all appropriate)

Tomato		Cauliflower		Spinach		Onion	
Green Chillies		Cabbage		Cilantro (Coriander)		Garlic	
Eggplant		Broccoli		Other leafy vegetables		Carrot	
Okra						Radish	
Pumpkin							
Gourds							
Cucumber							
Green Pepper							
Parval/Patal							
Others, please specify							

14.2.2 Fruits

(Tick all appropriate)

Banana		Orange		Apple		Watermelon		Grapes	
Mango		Lemons and limes		Pear		Cantaloupe		Gooseberry ('*amla*')	
Papaya		Kinnow		Peach				Strawberry	
Guava				Plum				Mulberry	
Pineapple									
Others, please specify									

15. Please answer the following questions:

Please note that this survey excludes the intake of potatoes and other starchy tubers such as cassava ('arabi'), sweet potato etc. in your diet.

15.1 In a typical week, on how many days do you eat fruits?		Number of days:	
15.2 How many servings of fruit do you eat in one day? (see Show Card)		Number of servings:	
15.3 Which form do you consume fruits in? (Tick all appropriate)	a.	Freshly cut	
	b.	Juice	
	c.	Canned	
	d.	Others, please specify	
15.4 During which part of the day are you most likely to consume fruits? (Tick all appropriate)	a.	Breakfast	
	b.	Lunch	
	c.	Dinner	
	d.	Others (such as mid-day, evening), please specify	
15.5 In a typical week, on how many days do you eat vegetables?		Number of days:	
15.6 How many servings of vegetables do you eat in a day? (see Show Card)		Number of servings:	
	a.	Chopped raw (salad)	
15.7 Which form do you consume vegetables in? (Tick all appropriate)	b.	Cooked	
	c.	Juice (such as carrot or tomato juice)	
	d.	Others, please specify	
15.8 During which part of the day are you most likely to consume vegetables? (Tick all appropriate)	a.	Breakfast	
	b.	Lunch	
	c.	Dinner	
	d.	Others (such as mid-day, evening), please specify	

15.9 Typically, which of the following vegetables do you consume?

(*Tick all appropriate*)

a. Group I		*b. Group II*		*c. Group III*		*d. Group IV*	
Tomato		Cauliflower		Spinach		Onion	
Green Chillies				Cilantro (Coriander)		Garlic	
Eggplant		Cabbage		Other leafy vegetables, please specify ________		Carrot	
Okra		Broccoli				Radish	
Pumpkin							
Gourds							
Cucumber							
Green Pepper							
Parval/Patal							
Total		Total		Total		Total	

e. Others, please specify:

15.10 Typically, which of the following fruits do you consume?

(*Tick all appropriate*)

Group I		*Group II*		*Group III*		*Group IV*		*Group V*	
Banana		Orange		Apple		Watermelon		Grapes	
Mango		Lemons and limes		Pear		Cantaloupe		Gooseberry ('*amla*')	
Papaya		Kinnow		Peach				Strawberry	
Guava				Plum				Mulberry	
Pineapple									
Total		Total		Total		Total		Total	

Others, please specify:

15.11 Typically, which of the following spices did you consume?

(*Tick all appropriate*)

a.	Ginger		b.	Turmeric	
c.	Cumin seed ('*jeera*')		d.	Clove	
e.	Mustard seed		f.	Black or white pepper	
g.	Poppy seed ('*khus-khus*')		h.	Red chilli powder	
i.	Others, please specify:				

III. Your Health Regime and Indicators

16. Tobacco consumption:

	Tick as appropriate	
a. Do you currently smoke/chew any tobacco products (e.g., cigarette, *bidi*, *hookah* etc)?	Yes	
(If No, go to Question 17)	No	
b. If yes, do you consume tobacco products regularly?	Yes	
	No	

17. Alcohol consumption:

		Tick as appropriate
17.1 Have you consumed alcohol in the last 12 months?	Yes	
(If No, go to Question 18)	No	
17.2 If yes, how frequently have you consumed at least one drink?	5-7 days/week	
	1-4 days/week	
	1-3 days/month	
	Less than once per month	

18. About your general health:

					Tick as appropriate	
18.1	How would you rate your physical health today? (1 - Highest; 5 - Lowest)	1. I am very healthy and feel excellent.	2. I am reasonably healthy and feel very good.	3. I am fairly healthy and feel good.	4. I am in poor health and feel bad.	5. I am in very poor health and feel very bad.
18.2	Do you spend time doing any physical activity during the week? (If No, go to Question 18.3)	Yes				
		No				
18.2.1	If yes, please specify the activity you engage in with the frequency.		Activity	Daily	More than 4 days per week	Less than 4 days per week
		18.1.	Yoga			
		18.2.	Running / jogging			
		18.3.	Brisk walking			
		18.4.	Workout at gymnasium			
		18.5.	Others, please specify ________			
18.3	Are you suffering from any health issue(s)? (If No, go to Question 19)	Yes				
		No				
18.3.1	If yes, please specify the health issue(s) you suffer from. (Tick all appropriate)	a	Low immunity			
		b.	Diabetes			
		c.	High Cholesterol			
		d.	High Blood Pressure			
		e.	Poor vision			
		f.	Heart diseases			
		g.	Obesity			
		h.	Low weight			
		i.	Skin diseases			
		j.	Digestive problems			
		k.	Bone weakness (e.g. Arthritis)			
		l.	High uric acid (e.g. Gout)			
		m.	Cancer			
		n.	Alzheimer's disease			
			Others, please specify ________			

IV. What determines your choice and purchase of fruits and vegetables?

19. Criteria and preferences for purchase of fruits and vegetables:

				Tick as appropriate
19.1	What are your criteria for purchasing fruits and vegetables? (Tick all appropriate)	19.1.	Quality/Freshness/Cleanliness	
		19.2.	Brand	
		19.3.	Chemical content	
		19.4.	Price	
		19.5.	Packaging	
		19.6.	Colour	
		19.7.	Flavour	
		19.8.	Do not know	
		19.9.	Others, please specify ________	
19.2	Which of the following would you prefer?		Organic	
			Inorganic	
19.2.1	Reason(s) for your preference:			
19.3	Which of the following would you prefer?		Branded	
			Unbranded	
19.3.1	Reason(s) for your preference:			
19.4	Would you be willing to pay a higher price for food items of your preference:		Yes	
			No	

V. Your General Awareness

20. Your awareness of benefits of consuming fruits and vegetables:

				Tick as appropriate
20.1	Are you aware of the benefits of consuming fruits and vegetables?		Yes	
			No	
20.1.1	If yes, what are the top 3 benefits? (Write briefly)			
20.1.2	What is your source of information? (Tick all appropriate)	20.1.	Print media: newspapers, magazines, etc.	
		20.2.	Electronic media: TV, radio, etc.	
		20.3.	Medical journals	
		20.4.	Medical practitioners	
		20.5.	Others, please specify ________	
20.2	Were you aware (before filling this questionnaire) that the WHO recommends consumption of at least 5 servings of fruits and vegetables daily? (See Show Card)		Yes	
			No	
20.2.1	Do you think that you are meeting the recommendation of consuming at least 5 fruits and vegetables daily? (See Show Card)		Yes	
			No	
20.2.2	If no, what are your reasons for the shortfall in intake? (Tick all appropriate)	a.	Cost is high	
		b.	Lifestyle issues: More convenient to eat fast foods, do not have time to cook	
		c.	Do not like fruits and vegetables	
		d.	Quality available is poor	
		e.	You perceive fruits and vegetables to have low nutritional content	
		f.	Seasonal availability	
		g.	Market location in inconvenient	
		h.	Storage capacity at home is limited	
		i.	Others, please specify ________	
20.2.3	How much do you think your daily intake of fruits and vegetables is? (See Show-card)		Less than 1	
			1–2	
			2–3	
			3–4	
			4–5	
			Above 5	

21. Your awareness of chemical content and pesticides in fruits and vegetables:

21.1	Are you aware of any of the following adulterants used in the production and sale of fruits and vegetables?	(Tick all appropriate)
a.	Pesticides (to kill insects etc.)	
b.	Urea and/or other chemical fertilisers	
c.	Carbide ('*masala*') for artificial ripening	
d.	Colour and/or Wax for enhancing appearance	
e.	Saw dust/sand/dirt in ground spices	
f.	Foreign leaves in leafy vegetables	
g.	Not aware of any	
h.	Others, please specify ____________	

21.2	How does such awareness affect your purchase and consumption of fruits and vegetables?	(Tick as appropriate)
a.	Purchase only organic products	
b.	Purchase from select outlets/retailers	
c.	Purchase canned and branded products	
d.	Consume after thorough cleaning	
e.	Consume only cooked vegetables and peeled fruits	
f.	Not affected at all	
g.	Others, please specify________	

22. Policy and Regulatory Awareness:

			Tick as appropriate
22.1	Are you aware of your rights as specified in the Consumer Protection Act, 1986?	Yes	
		No	
22.2	Are you aware of the food safety regulations as per the Food Safety and Standards Act (FSSA), 2006, in the country?	Yes	
		No	

23. Policy recommendations:

In your opinion, what should the government do to address the following issues:		
23.1	Food safety standards	
23.2	Consumer awareness and information dissemination	
23.3	Reduction of food inflation	
23.4	Quality of food items	
23.5	Accessibility and availability of food items	

VI. About Nutrition Supplements

24. Health and nutrition supplements:

		Tick as appropriate
24.1 Are you currently using any health and nutritional supplement(s) in your diet?	Yes	
	No	
24.2 If yes, please mention names of products used:		
24.3 Are you aware of any of the following brands of food supplements available in the market? (Tick all appropriate)	Himalaya	
	Shree Baidyanath Ayurved	
	Amway Nutrilite	
	Dabur	
	Vista Nutrition	
	Zenith Nutrition	
	Emami	
	Herbalife	
	Others, please specify ________	
24.4 Where would you like to purchase food supplements? (Tick all appropriate)	Nearby general stores	
	Supermarket/ Hypermarket	
	Online stores	
	Teleshopping	
	Pharmacy	
	Direct sellers	
	Others, please specify ________________	

25. Any other comments you would like to add:

Thank you for your cooperation in completing this questionnaire.

Show-card:

WHO Standards for One Serving of Fruits and Vegetables

In general, one serving of vegetables is considered to be one bowl (80 grams) of raw green leafy vegetables such as spinach or salad; one half cup (80 grams) of other vegetables cooked or chopped raw, such as tomato, carrot, pumpkin, corn, cabbage, beans or onion; or one half cup (80 grams) of vegetable juice such as tomato or carrot juice.

Likewise, one serving of fruit is considered to be one medium sized fruit such as an apple, banana or orange; one half cup (80 grams) chopped, cooked or canned fruit; or one half cup (80 grams) of fruit juice such as orange or mixed fruit juice.

All forms of fruits and vegetables such as fresh, frozen, raw and cooked are considered.

Following is a pictorial description of the World Health Organization (WHO) recommended serving size of fruits and vegetables.

Appendix D

Sample Distribution

Figure D.1

Distribution of Sample by Education Levels

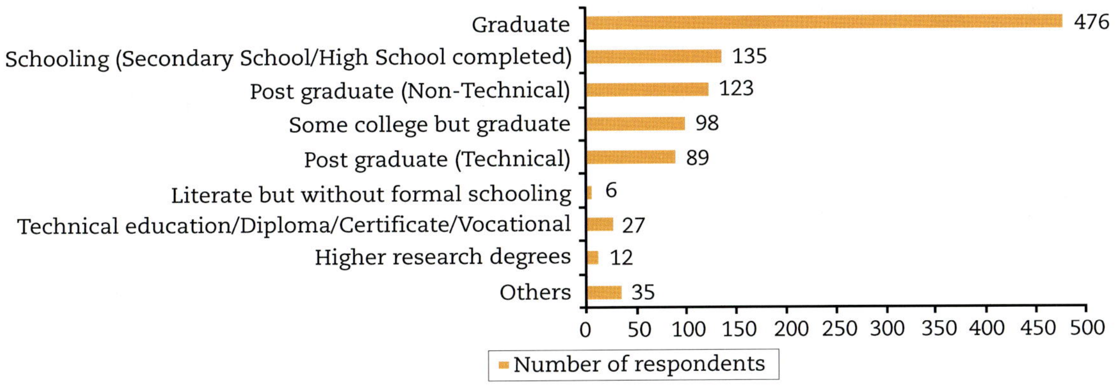

Source: Authors' calculations.

Figure D.2

Distribution of Sample by Occupation

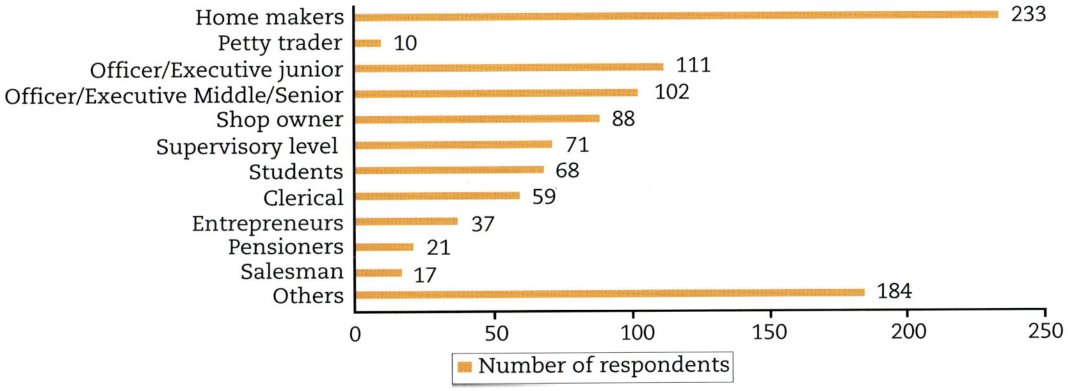

Source:Authors' calculations.

Figure D.3

Mean Number of Members and Earning Members in a Family across Cities

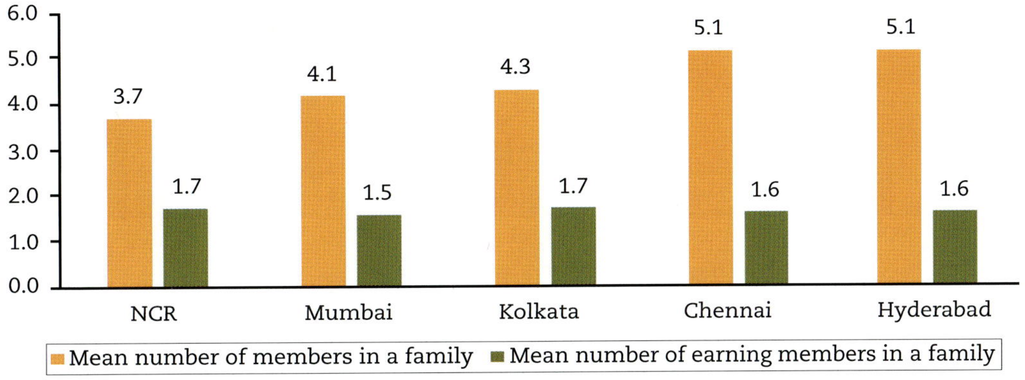

Source: Authors' calculations.

Figure D.4

Distribution of Family Structure across Cities

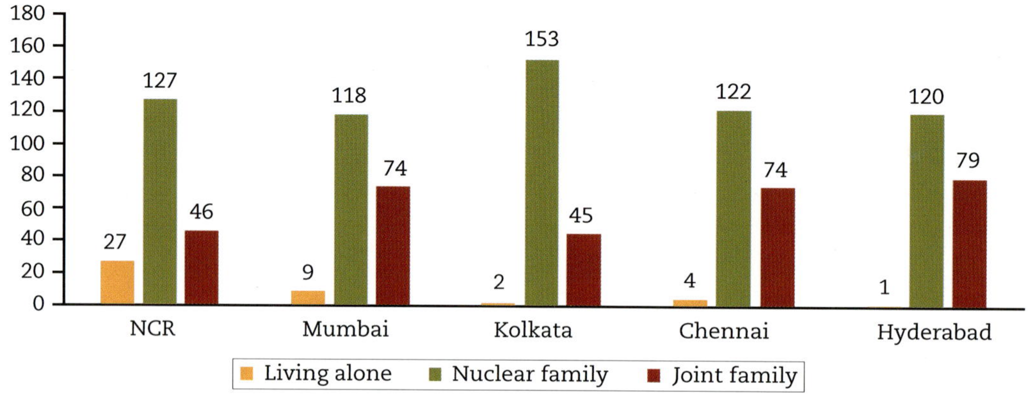

Source: Authors' calculations.

Figure D.5

Distribution of Respondents having Fruits by Number of Days in a Week across Cities (in numbers)

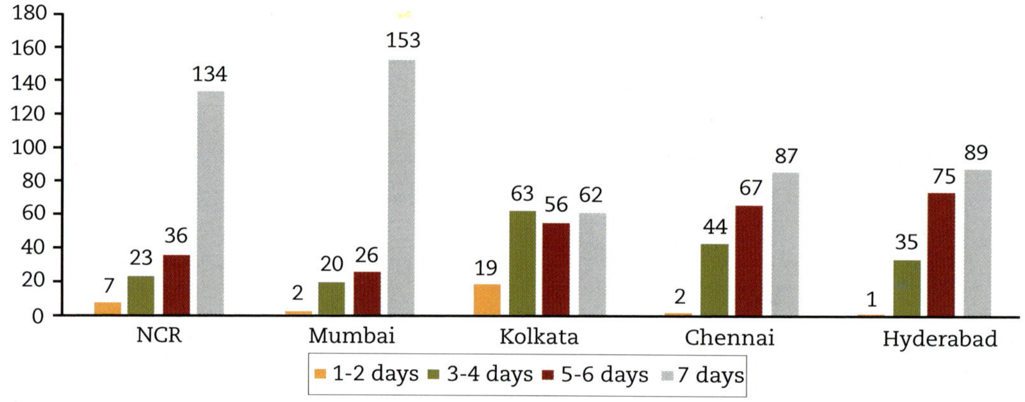

Source: Authors' calculations.

Figure D.6

Distribution of Respondents having Vegetables by Number of Days in a Week across Cities (in numbers)

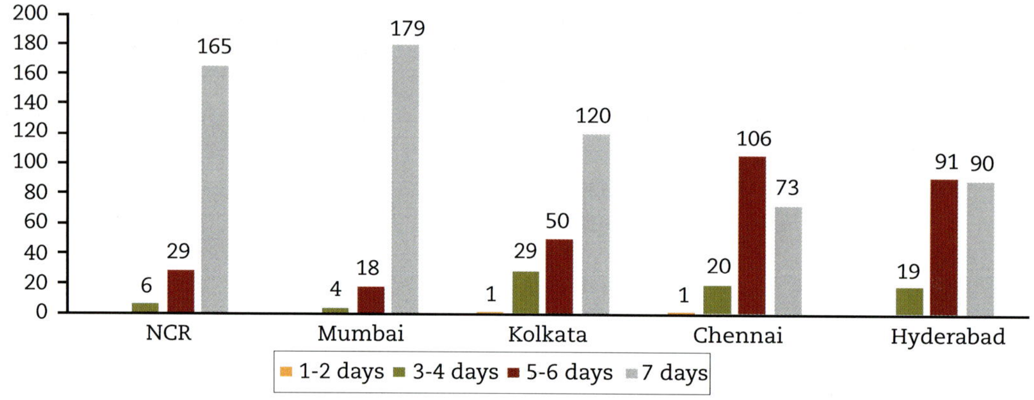

Source: Authors' calculations.

Appendix E

Regression Analysis

In this section, we provide a regression analysis of the data. The regression results confirm our findings. We do a linear regression using the Ordinary Least Squares (OLS) method. The regression specification is given by

$$Y = \alpha + \beta X + \varepsilon$$

where Y is the dependent variable and X is the set of independent variables. α is the constant term, β are the coefficients of the independent variables and ε is the error term.

The dependent variable in the regression analysis is *total serving* and measures the total serving of fruits and vegetables.

The independent variables considered are:

(a) *Age-Group* captures the age bracket.

(b) *AnnualHHsIncome* measures the total annual income of the household.

(c) *HHsMembers_No* measures the numbers of members in the household.

(d) *male* is a dummy variable and takes value 1 if gender is male.

(e) *veg* is a dummy variable and takes value 1 if diet type is vegetarian.[1]

(f) *housewifedummy* is a dummy variable and takes value 1 if occupation is housewife.

(g) *studentdummy* is a dummy variable and takes value 1 if occupation is student.

(h) *house-helpdummy* is a dummy variable and takes value 1 if fruits and vegetables are purchased by the house-help.

(i) *dietersdummy* is a dummy variable and takes value 1 if the respondent has a dietary restriction or an allergy.

(j) *NCRdummy, bomdummy, koldummy and chendummy* are dummy variables and takes value 1 if the location is NCR, Mumbai, Kolkata and Chennai respectively.

We have four model specifications in the regression analysis. This is to capture whether the intake of fruits and vegetables differ significantly across gender, diet type, occupation of respondents and location. Regression Table E.1 below gives the regression results. In Models 1, 2 and 3, we do not include the location dummies. In Model 4, we have the location dummies to capture location specific effects. As clearly seen, annual household income has a positive impact on the total intake of fruits and vegetables. The coefficient is positive and significant for *AnnualHHsIncome* in all the models pecifications. The intake of fruits and vegetables is significantly higher for the vegetarians. The coefficient for *veq* is positive and significant. Housewives on an average consume more while students consume less than the average. *housewifedummy* is positive and significant while the *studentdummy* is also significant and negative. Dietary restrictions and whether house-helps purchase fruits and vegetables have no impact on the total intake as seen in Model 4. The coefficients for *house-helpdummy* and *dietersdummy* are both insignificant. In Models 1 and 2, the higher the age group, the greater is the consumption of fruits and vegetables, while the coefficient loses its significance in Model 3 and Model 4. As seen from Model 4, there is something inherent to a location, primarily the kind of cuisine they have, that determines the intake of fruits and vegetables. For example, Kolkata has the least intake of fruits and vegetables and this can be attributed to the fact that consumers in Kolkata are more likely to have more fish and meat and eat less of fruits and vegetables.

1. Jain and vegetarian are clubbed as vegetarian while eggetarian and non-vegetarian has been clubbed as non-vegetarian. Results do not change even if we treat them separately.

Regression Table E.1

	(1) *Totalserving*	(2) *Totalserving*	(3) *Totalserving*	(4) *Totalserving*
Age_Group	0.115** (3.05)	0.0805** (2.22)	0.0475 (1.14)	-0.00140 (-0.04)
Annual_HHs_Income	0.248*** (7.04)	0.228*** (6.43)	0.224*** (6.09)	0.236*** (6.83)
male	-0.0899 (-1.16)			
HHs_Members_No		0.0364* (2.12)	0.0480** (2.73)	-0.0126 (-0.79)
veg		0.620*** (8.31)		0.503*** (6.72)
housewifedummy			0.181* (1.97)	
studentdummy			-0.442** (-2.65)	
house-helpdummy				0.106 (0.96)
dietersdummy				0.0955 (0.87)
NCRdummy				-0.693*** (-6.08)
bomdummy				-0.817*** (-7.27)
koldummy				-0.893*** (-7.51)
chendummy				0.405*** (3.85)
Constant	2.694*** (20.20)	2.353*** (17.25)	2.652*** (17.30)	3.199*** (20.23)
N	1001	1001	1001	1001

Note: t statistics in parentheses; *<0.05, **<0.01, ***<0.001.

Since age in this survey age was recorded in intervals, the variable *Age_Group* would capture the linear effects. Hence, to capture the age group effects, we introduce dummies *age 1, age 2, age 3 and age 4* which will take value 1 if the age group is between 18-25 years, 25-35 years, 35-50 years and 50-60 years respectively. The results are presented in Regression Table E.2. With age dummies, we find the trend similar to that presented in Regression Table E.1. The coefficients for *age3* and *age4* are positive and significant in most cases indicating that individuals in the age group above 35 years have significantly more fruits and vegetables compared to the average. The coefficient for *age1* is not significant but negative in all models expect Model 4, indicating that the younger generation are having less fruits and vegetables than the average. The coefficient for annual household income is positive and significant in all models and shows that income plays a very important role in determining the intake of fruits and vegetables. Here the *studentdummy* and *housewifedummy* loses its significance (see model 3) though the coefficients are in the right direction. Coefficients for *house-helpdummy* and *dietersdummy* are insignificant indicating that purchases made by house-help or not and having a dietary restriction does not play an important role in determining the intake of fruits and vegetables. Location plays an important role and is captured in Model 4 where we introduce the location dummies.

Regression Table E.2

	(1) *Totalserving*	(2) *Totalserving*	(3) *Totalserving*	(4) *Totalserving*
Age1	-0.200 (-0.97)	-0.0987 (-0.50)	-0.139 (-0.59)	0.0198 (0.11)
Age2	0.279 (1.51)	0.313 (1.76)	0.272 (1.48)	0.207 (1.28)
Age3	0.556** (3.05)	0.558** (3.18)	0.523** (2.88)	0.243 (1.50)
Age4	0.406* (2.07)	0.374* (1.98)	0.368 (1.88)	0.126 (0.73)
Annual_HHs_Income	0.241*** (2.07)	0.226*** (6.43)	0.216*** (5.88)	0.234*** (6.76)
Male	-0.0736 (-0.96)			
HHs_Members_No		0.0305 (1.80)	0.0458** (2.62)	-0.0128 (-0.80)
Veg		0.609*** (8.25)		0.507*** (6.77)
housewifedummy			0.123 (1.34)	
studentdummy			-0.0611 (-0.29)	
NCRdummy				-0.651*** (-5.61)
bomdummy				-0.786*** (-6.93)
koldummy				-0.843*** (-6.99)
chendummy				0.392*** (3.73)
house-helpdummy				0.119 (1.07)
dietersdummy				0.114 (1.04)
Constant	2.676*** (13.95)	2.253*** (12.15)	2.475*** (12.99)	2.995*** (15.38)
N	1001	1001	1001	1001

Note: t statistics in parentheses; *<0.05, **<0.01, ***<0.001.

Appendix F

Health Condition of Respondents

Of the total number of respondents, 424 (42.3 per cent) have health issues while the rest do not have any health issue. Health issues are more prevalent in the higher age group. Only 16.8 per cent of the respondents in the age group 18-25 years have health issues, while 23.3 per cent in the age group 25-35 years, 49.7 per cent of the respondents in the age group 35-50 years, 69.6 per cent in the age group 50-60 years and 72.9 per cent who are aged above 60 years have health issues. Out of 424 respondents, 290 (68.4 per cent) have a single health issue while the rest 134 (31.4 per cent) have multiple health issues. Figure F.1 provides the frequency of different health issues across the sample. Poor vision is the most common health issue followed by blood pressure and high uric acid.

Figure F.1

Distribution of Sample according to Health Issues

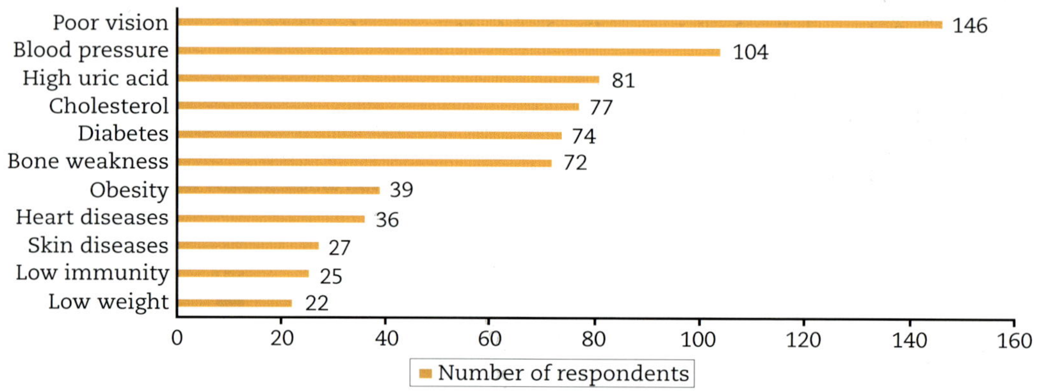

Source: Authors' calculations

The number of respondents indulging in some physical activity is 402 (40.2 per cent); the rest 599 do not do any physical activity. Out of those who do physical activity, 300 (74.6 per cent) perform single activity while the rest 102 (25.4 per cent) are involved in multiple activities. Table F.1 gives the frequency of different physical activities undertaken.

Table F.1

Frequency of Physical Activities Undertaken

Activity	*More than 4 days a week*	*Less than 4 days a week*	*Daily*
Yoga	16	14	44
Running/Jogging	63	25	47
Brisk walking	58	20	68
Gym workout	45	14	18

Source: Authors' calculations

In the sample, 161 (16.1 per cent) respondents reported that they are healthy and feel excellent, 536 (53.5 per cent) reported they are reasonably healthy and feel very good, 275 (27.5 per cent) are fairly healthy and only 47 feel they have poor health and feel bad. There is no one who feels they have very poor health and feel very bad.

Of the 1001 respondents, 278(27.8 per cent) smoke/chew any tobacco product and out of 278, 245 (88.1 per cent) do it regularly. Respondents in the age group 18-25 years are least prone to smoking/chewing tobacco products (11.5 per cent), while the proportion of respondents who smoke/chew tobacco products are not significantly different across other age groups. 30 per cent of the respondents in the age group above 25 years smoke/chew tobacco products.

The number of respondents who consume alcohol is 228 (22.8 per cent). Out of those who consume alcohol, 18 (7.9 per cent) consume on 5-7 days/week, 62 consume (27.2 per cent) on 1-4 days/week while 82 (35.9 per cent) consume 1-3 days/month and the rest 66 (28.9 per cent) consume less than once per month. While only 8 per cent of the respondents in the age group 18-25 years consume alcohol, 24.5 per cent of the respondents in the age group above 35 years do so.